Voyage of Learning

My Years Learning, Teaching and Enabling

Voyage of Learning

My Years Learning, Teaching and Enabling

MIND-TREK

Mind-Trek Series
Book 1

Dr. M. V. PRASAD

EXCELLER BOOKS®
A GLOBAL PRESS

Voyage of Learning
My Years Learning, Teaching and Enabling

Cover by Exceller Books using resources from Pixabay.com

ISBN: 978-93-48892-47-8

First published in India in 2025 by Exceller Books,
An imprint of GE Group

Address: G1, Dream Apartment, Degree College Road, Belgharia,
Kolkata, 700056, India
www.excellerbooks.com

EXCELLER BOOKS®
A GLOBAL PRESS

Acknowledgements

I wish to express my sincere gratitude to all those who inspired, motivated, coached, critiqued, taught, listened to, and shared with me during this wondrous journey of which I was fortunate to be a part. Inspiration often came from the most unexpected quarters when one was least expecting it, and one was reminded to be open, vulnerable, humble and gracious at all times!

I would like to especially thank my parents, who instilled in me a value system and a sense of fairness that has remained with me to this day. Finding J. Krishnamurti was a turning point in my life for which I am eternally grateful. I am also thankful to all my students, fellow teachers, school administrator friends and parents in all the places I worked – Rishi Valley, Bharatiya Vidya Bhavan in Baroda, Indian School in Bahrain and The Daly College in Indore, who taught me much more than they might realise! I would like to specifically mention a few people who enriched me and helped shape me over the years - S. Balasundaram, S. Ramakrishnan, N.S. Ganesh, Swami Hariprasaddasji, Anil Malhotra, S.V. Narasimhan, M.P. Chhaya, B.K. Sood and S.D. Singh. My sincere thanks to Anil Sharma for encouraging me to write this book and for all his help in bringing this effort to fruition. I also wish to express my gratitude to P. Mukherjee for his help throughout the publication process. I also gratefully acknowledge the efforts of Stephen Bohannon in helping us design the front cover of this book.

Finally, I would like to acknowledge my co-traveller and friend, my wife, Sheela, whose love, strength, wisdom, and companionship have carried me further than anything else in life. She taught me much about myself and the world, and I am thankful for our lifetime together. To Priya, Srinadh, Gaurang, Sunita, Ashutosh, Aishwarya, Ananya, Anika and Aanya – thank you for giving me the strength and energy to complete this book!

Table of Contents

Series Editor's Note by P. Mukherjee

Imagination is more important than knowledge. Knowledge is limited. Imagination encircles the world.

— Albert Einstein

An idea that is developed and put into action is more important than an idea that exists only as an idea.

— Gautama the Buddha

As we embark on a journey of a trilogy of books as a part of the Mind-Trek series and the first book is firmly planted in your hands, let me begin by invoking a timeless piece of wisdom that Gandhiji always refers to: Be the Change.

Hence, these three books (the first of which you have in your hands now) would serve as an invaluable record and an oral history of field experiences of three contemporary legends of education, legends who embodied the idea of being the change.

As they say, the first seeds of change are planted during school life. School life is a combination of an idea of developing processes and praxis for observing, decoding, understanding, studying, researching, unlearning-learning-re-learning, discussing, debating and building a working consensus, keeping in mind that everyone comes from a different milieu, and everyone will not have the same socio-cultural orientation towards goals, ambitions and life skills.

How do we, therefore, achieve this idea of self-development-at-your-own-pace as a goal?

We cannot and should not JUDGE THIS process of self-development from the prism of the success of a few individual students seeking higher examination ranks and the teaching staff blindly supporting that dream.

And in the process/therefore, vindicating methods such as rote learning, punishing tuition schedule, litany of period tests and rote recall as the success mantras.

That is far from the real deal.

The real deal is the question: what should be the yardstick for measuring the overall growth index of a child?

I firmly believe that the answer lies in looking at the ways and means to identify the areas of passion lying deep inside every student. This passion dictates the goal, not vice versa, as is prevalent in most institutions now.

In a society where market forces define tectonic changes in technology, social priorities, family structures, the overarching reach of social media, and the choice of careers, there is a complex set of parental and societal ambitions thrust onto the child.

It is important for us as educators to define the growth curve, understand these challenges, and make constant course corrections in the running of schools.

The chronicle of any institution is not about the achievement of any one person or one batch, no matter how gifted or brilliant the individual or the group is.

It is about sharing and appreciating the power of many distinct voices.

The prosperity and peace of our future will depend on the "distinct" voice and the skills that you and your generation will strive to bring into your lives and, consequently, into the lives of others.

As flows of information, materials, and capital move around the globe at ever-oscillating loops and as the new regulatory policies and international agreements impact educational journeys and society at large, our old assumptions of stability and order are severely challenged.

We must all develop critical thinking skills and a strong knowledge base to become a humane leader in such an environment.

Gandhiji wrote: *'It has been my experience that I am always true from my point of view, and am often wrong from the point of view of my honest critics. I know we are both right from our respective points of view."*

When you truly listen to other people and try to understand their way of seeing the world, you can learn the wisdom Gandhiji expressed in his life, actions, and words.

Please remember that you are here to share your ideas and dilemmas. It's your sincerity and thoughtfulness which are important. Rest is immaterial.

In all these journeys, we have got to remember that the child is at the centre of any programme. A child is both the fulcrum and the crux. In these evolving times and rapidly changing cultural mores, we should always keep the child's inquiry and learning at the epicentre of our practices.

Dr. M.V Prasad's book, which will be the first in our trilogy of books as a part of the "Mind-Trek" series, is a meditation and a musing about finding one's voice in the din of educational expectations.

The remarkable candour in this book and the nuggets of wisdom on every page are testimonies of a distinct voice that seeks to stitch past learnings with a contemporary worldview.

As we wade into the choppy waters of the complex analogue then versus the even more complex digital present now, let's remember A. N Whitehead's remark: *Learning preserves errors of the past as well as its wisdom.*

Dr. Prasad's musings are exactly that: discussing the nuances of the past along with delving into dilemmas of the present to forge an idea of a better, sustainable and more humane future.

Easier said than done, but this invaluable documentation by Dr Prasad emphasises the idea of a necessary utopia that we should all strive for.

Dr. Prasad is a chronicler of that necessary and urgent utopia that most miss out on.

Varanasi
May 23, 2025

Foreword by M. V. Prasad

Every journey is unique and special, often full of surprises, plenty of excitement, and occasional moments of doubt. Every now and then, we find ourselves lost when navigating to a new place, and more often than not, we eventually figure it out! Strangers that we least expected help us along, and we discover the most amazing richness in places we least expected. Our preconceived notions about a place or its people are shattered.

Sometimes, we realize that the destination we had in mind was as majestic as we had imagined, and other times, we remember the journey much more than the destination we had set out to conquer and the co-travelers we met, traveled with, learned from, and parted who enriched us and taught us about the world and ourselves.

And what of the journey within that each of us must undertake – to observe, listen, discover, and make peace with – that inner self?

Thus, my journey of almost 50 years in the field of education has been a wondrous ride, full of inspiring people I learnt from, observed, marveled at, was intrigued by, and, in some small way, perhaps influenced a little!

It also was not the journey I had in mind for myself when I was in my 20s, but one that I am deeply thankful for. Every part of it - from my formative years, observing and being influenced by my inspiring father and my strong and steadfast mother, to my college years, full of hope and possibilities, to my years in Rishi Valley, beginning with a chance encounter with JK that set me upon this unexpected but deeply rewarding path of becoming a teacher, surrounded by children and the possibilities they represent and eventually becoming a leader of multiple institutions of learning, traveling the world and getting to do it all on a scale I had never imagined for myself.

But while every journey is unique and personal and one that each of us has to go through for ourselves, what is also true is that the paths that others have taken inform us and make us aware of pitfalls and possibilities that might lie in wait for us, giving us a loose framework to benefit from.

This is the spirit in which I write this book. It is not meant to be a roadmap or a book of recipes for other administrators, teachers, parents, or children. I have tried to capture my insights, experiences, reflections, and recollections of what I saw, heard, learned, observed, and dwelled upon over the decades. This book does not claim to have all the answers, nor does it pose all the questions one needs to ponder.

That said, at various moments in my career, I wish I could have drawn upon the experience or counsel of those who came before me. This is especially so in the field of school education in India, where being a school Principal is often a thankless job—where everyone thinks they know how to do what you do. Still, nobody truly can relate to the unique challenges and situations you find yourself in.

I often wished more books had been written by former heads of schools and former teachers, just as budding corporate leaders, aspiring sports personalities, and those pursuing public life always had a plethora of literature and wisdom to draw upon!

Every school Principal stays up at night wondering if they are striking the right balance between fostering a culture of innovation and preserving a sense of timeless traditions; achieving the ideal mixture of academics, sports, and the arts; managing to emphasize a spirit of healthy competition but learning to win with humility and lose with grace; creating an environment where children feel valued and loved but are not filled with entitlement, where parents are partners but not overbearing, where teachers feel like they are set up to succeed even while allowing each of them to leave their unique footprint and so on.

There is not a definitive manual one can read, nor should there be one! But we should be able to draw upon how others grappled with these questions, what worked for them and what did not, and how the next generation can be just a little wiser as a result! That is not to say I was deprived of this opportunity altogether. I have learnt much in the interactions I was fortunate to have with other leaders, teachers, parents, and children in the schools where I taught and led. I also had the opportunity to listen to, interact with, and seek counsel from many at the Indian Public Schools Conference (IPSC) or the numerous internal conferences I was fortunate to have attended, in addition to several in-service training programmes I was part of.

However, for a field that involves so much reading and writing, the body of written literature in school education, especially in an Indian context, is relatively thin! And so, I was especially motivated to document my journey as an educationist and teacher in the hope that it is just one among many such works that deepen and strengthen our collective understanding.

More than anything else, I look at this effort as doing my part in a collective and long relay race – where each of us runs our leg to the very best of our abilities and passes on the baton to the next generation of thinkers, educators, and leaders to enrich our understanding further, appreciate and help us navigate a new set of contradictions and provide some guidance on how to continue the endless process of shaping happy children, who pursue excellence, who embody a spirit of curiosity and who help us make this world a little better.

SECTION I

The Foundations

|Chapter 1|

Early Years: School, Friends, and Family

As I sit back and reflect on where it all began, I recollect the earliest images and memories imprinted in my mind.

It was 1943, and I was five when we lived in a town called Pithapuram in the East Godavari District of Andhra Pradesh. It was time for me to start attending school. Soon after, a ceremony called "AKSHARABHYASAM" was held at home in the company of family, close friends, and relatives. I started school in Grade 1 (there was no kindergarten back then), and I do not recall crying or expressing fear or apprehension about leaving home for a few hours daily. I wonder whether that was because I was naturally drawn to be around and learn in the company of others or whether it was because education was ingrained somehow within us, given that my father was in the field – he was the Inspector of Schools for the district.

Our first-grade teacher was kind and loving. We loved him dearly, and we learned the alphabet and numbers in this happy environment. Just as everything was going perfectly as far as I was concerned, a month after that, my father was transferred! This would be the first of several moves he and we would make, and I learned at an early age about change being the only constant in life! It turned out that he was transferred to Narasapuram in West Godavari District, a lovely town on the banks of the Godavari River. I ended up getting admitted into Grade 2 in a school there, thanks in part to my Grade 1 schooling in Pithapuram.

The early 1940s were a time when massive changes were sweeping through India and the world. WWII was reaching its end game after years of fierce fighting and the attendant human toll. No part of the world was untouched in the wake of these events. As it turned out, Indian independence from British rule was also around the corner after decades of struggle. Of course, at that time, kids of my age did not really know or appreciate the significance of all these things, but we would watch and marvel at the sight of seaplanes that would land in the Godavari River carrying soldiers, primarily British and leave again after a few hours. Soldiers would walk around the town with a sense of authority and the policemen were deferential and respectful to them. One day, I remember my elder brother commenting: "Their days of ruling over us are nearing their end, and all these English people will soon go back to their country." It was 1944, and my brother and father often discussed the end of the war and the onset of freedom for India.

On a personal front, in what was now becoming a regular feature, my father was transferred again – this time to Guntur, a flourishing city a little away from the Krishna River. Thus, I was admitted into Grade 3 in a very good school in Guntur. It was here that I first started learning English in addition to Telugu, Arithmetic, Nature Study and Art. We had an excellent teacher who taught us English. The way he introduced the alphabet was quite interesting, and it helped us read and write small words. This is something I recall clearly even today! In retrospect, I am convinced that it was this 3rd-grade teacher of mine who created in me a love for the subject, which, in the years to come, became my passion for life. I remember his name, Mr. Narasimha Rao, 75 years on! I am filled with gratitude for this great teacher and wish he could hear me say this wherever he is. It was Henry Adams who said: "A teacher affects eternity; one can never tell where the influence stops."

Even as my third-grade teacher was making a lifelong mark on me, I was all the while learning, as a great Greek philosopher supposedly said, about how change was the only constant in life! As I was finishing my third grade, my father was transferred again, this time as Headmaster of a Teacher Training School in Bheemunipatnam, a seaside resort town near Visakhapatnam. The British shortened the names to Bimli and Vizag, respectively. Bimli is a picturesque little waterfront town surrounded by hills. The town itself is on a slope with a temple on the hill and below it was my father's institute. I recall vividly that when it rained, the entire town would get cleaned by the water flowing down into the sea. I studied Grades IV, V and VI in the local High School. When I was 9 years old and in Grade 4, India formally attained Independence in August 1947, and there was unlimited jubilation all around. Classes were cancelled for a whole week. We would assemble at school in the morning, pick up Indian flags and go around town shouting the slogan "Swatantra Bharat Ki Jai, Mahatma Gandhi ki Jai." (Glory to Independent India, glory to Mahatma Gandhi). We would return after 2 or 3 hours, and our Headmaster or a visitor would speak to us about freedom and what it meant, and while we had a sense of what had just transpired, there was much spoken of which we could not understand a whole lot. Sweets would be distributed, and we would go home. My teachers would also talk about independence in classes, and everyone was happy that we were finally free and no longer ruled by a foreign power. One day, my father explained to me the significance of freedom, and thus, slowly, I began to appreciate what the celebrations were all about.

After getting promoted to District Education Officer (DEO), my father's next posting was at Bapatla, where I studied my 8th and 9th grades in high school. Although I enjoyed learning all the subjects, I was particularly interested in English and Mathematics. My father was deputed to go to Sevagram, near Wardha (Maharashtra), to undergo Basic Training for 6 months at the Gandhi Ashram there. My mother had to manage the household and all her children by herself, while my father would send money for our expenses every month. Since my mother had her hands full with all that she had to manage, I volunteered to help her manage the household finances, and she agreed since I had a reputation for being reliable and meticulous.

I would buy groceries, a daily stock of vegetables and whatever else my mother wanted and keep accounts scrupulously. I would also observe the utmost economy without sacrificing quality. This was something I had learnt by observing my parents, whose principle was to never stint on essentials required and also ensure there was no wastage. My mother and siblings were pleased with my ability to manage money. This experience implanted in me the values of living within one's means, no ostentation, but having the necessities to lead a simple, reasonably comfortable life and never spend more than what one earned, all the while setting aside whatever one could for a rainy day.

My father returned after his deputation period ended, and he had earned an additional qualification through his Basic Training. Almost as an immediate recognition, he was transferred as DEO of Machilipatnam (Masula), a larger town with historical significance and a port city 3 miles away from where we were then.

I did my classes 10 and 11 in the Hindu College High School, which is easily the best school I have attended. Those days, 11th grade was the year one took a Board Exam as India followed the system of 11 years of schooling called Secondary School Leaving Certificate (SSLC), followed by 2 years of "Intermediate" when one specialised in a group of subjects followed by a 2-year degree (11+2+2). I cleared my SSLC Public Exam and joined the Hindu College for my Intermediate programme. It was a wonderful college with excellent faculty. I was surrounded by many bright students, all eager to learn and grow.

And thus went the story of my early years – full of innocence, surrounded by some wonderful teachers, spent in the loving company of my friends, siblings, and parents who taught me so much in a multitude of ways – all of this at a time when India was finding its feet with visionary leaders like Nehru and Patel who had led the fight for freedom alongside Gandhi now laying the foundations upon which a strong, secular and democratic India would be built upon!

This was a time of great optimism and hope, with the future promising great possibilities, both personally and for our young country!

People

As I round out my early school years, I cannot help but think about the role that the people around me played during that period.

Two classmates of mine from those early years played an outstanding role in my growth and learning. GSR Sarma was in my class at school, and we subsequently studied together at Andhra University. He was a student of Mathematical Physics while I was doing my English Honours. He was a brilliant all-rounder and had an extraordinary penchant for English, and he would give me valuable feedback on my essays and, indeed, make them better. He subsequently went to Heidelberg University in Germany for his research and eventually joined the faculty there, where he went on to become a professor. It was not surprising to me that he became a world figure in Theoretical Physics and settled in Germany. Unfortunately, he recently passed away.

Another childhood friend and classmate was LSRK Sastry, who, too, attended school and, subsequently, university with me. He, too, joined English Honours. He possessed a rare felicity of expression and a beautiful style. He, Sarma and I shared a room in the hostel. Sastry helped me a lot in many ways - from explaining the deeper meaning of some poems to improving my essays. He became a Professor of English at the same Andhra University and attained global recognition. We stayed in touch through the decades and I visited him on several occasions until he, too, passed away a few years back.

By a happy coincidence, Sarma, Sastry, and I shared a journey that lasted many years. I remember the fun, enriching, and meaningful moments we shared during those important early and formative years. I am profoundly thankful to have met them and had the honour of being their co-traveller and friend.

Of course, I would be remiss if I did not talk briefly about my siblings and the happy childhood we shared in a happy home. Lakshmana Murty was our oldest sibling, and he was followed by my sister Uma Devi, and my two younger brothers Murali and Suryanarayana. We grew up in a harmonious and loving environment, and our relationships remained strong even as we followed our passions and vocations in geographically distant locations in the decades to come.

Finally, I turn to the two most important people in my life and the influence they had on shaping my character: my parents, of course.

My father was deeply influenced from childhood by his paternal uncle, a flourishing lawyer, erudite scholar, freedom fighter, and a highly respected person in society known for his simplicity, philanthropy, and fair play. My father would often say that it was his uncle who implanted in him these values that he would go on to live by and is remembered for to this day by those who knew him.

My parents, M. Nageswara Rao and Annapurnadevi (Baroda, Circa 1982)

He worked under British bosses until about 1946, and they respected him despite his wearing a traditional khadi dhoti and kurta, a nicely folded upper cloth, and a long coat if the occasion required. Knowing full well that he was a Gandhian, they appreciated him for his genuineness, uprightness, and principles.

He had a great admiration for Gandhiji right from his childhood. The Indian National Congress held its annual session in 1923 at Kakinada, in Andhra. He was then a college student at Vijayanagaram. He enrolled as a volunteer and went to Kakinada, 200 kilometres away. He was thrilled to see Gandhiji, Nehru, Sardar Patel and other leaders. He was given the duty of looking after Sarojini Naidu. My father would often recount his joy at seeing Gandhiji from close quarters, the affectionate way Sarojini Naidu would interact with him, and how happy she was when he told her that he had read most of her poems.

My father's work ethic won him respect from all quarters. A man of unquestioned integrity, he had his own take on rules. According to him, rules exist for a reason and should always be followed. However, if the administrator is vested with discretionary powers, he/she should interpret the rules creatively to help a person when all else is equal. The beneficiary should neither be a relative nor a person who is likely to help him in future. Then, it becomes *quid pro quo,* which is unethical. If he/she had to administer a punishment as per rules, he/she would do it calmly with no emotion. His principle was one should leave one's table clean before going home at the end of the day.

He would not accept any gifts from people connected with him officially. His children were treated like other children. He inspected our schools every year, but we kept our distance from him. We were not allowed to speak ill of any teacher. We would never visit him in the office, but on rare occasions when I dropped in to fill out a form or do similar work, I would enter his room when there was no one else there. I should mention in this context that I noticed he had two pots of ink (that was the time when fountain pens were not used widely—one would use felt pens and dip the nib in an ink bottle). He explained to me once that he used one ink bottle for official work and the other bottle, which he bought, for personal work. That was a practice which very few officials would follow. He would often tell his children that if an administrator functioned in a dispassionate manner following rules, he would have sound sleep at night.

My father was a deeply spiritual person and had reverence for all religions. He would confine his religious beliefs and practices to his home. He was a devotee of Lord Rama and spent all his time after retirement contributing articles on spiritual matters to journals. He was invited to be the President of Sri Ramanamakshetram, a unique institution dedicated to Lord Sri Ram at Guntur. It was a purely honorary post but he introduced proper systems and reorganised the administration of the institution. He edited their monthly journal and contributed an article a month on spiritual matters. Thus, he occupied himself in meaningful work after retirement.

He knew several stories drawn from classics from around the world, each with a moral. His grandchildren would flock around him and ask for stories he could narrate in an interesting manner. In later life, the children realised how the stories contributed to shaping their value system.

My father is a source of inspiration, wisdom, and strength for me to this day. It is no coincidence that I would go on to pursue a career in education. The values he so easily and faithfully lived help guide me every day of my life.

My mother was not educated in the traditional sense of going to school/college, but she was a highly gifted, intelligent woman who was a repository of practical wisdom. She could read and write Telugu, of course. She taught us the value and importance of being orderly, and after we returned from school, we would fold and keep the school uniform ready for the following day before retiring to bed. We were advised to always dress well but always simply and unostentatiously. She herself would cook our food, serve my father and us all, ensuring we ate well and she would be the last to have her food.

She never hesitated to point out our deficiencies and correct us when necessary. She provided a conducive atmosphere for all children to study at home. My father had to be out often at work, and she managed the home front most ideally. She ran the house with dignity, observing the economy and providing her children with all the necessities but with no wastage. She gave us a good foundation for leading our later lives with values. She brought us up on the right lines and provided a direction in life, firmly entrenched in values.

Years later, my siblings would tell me that they saw many of her traits in me, and I have, to this day, wondered if my mother could have been an administrator and leader of people in her own right with all the wonderful qualities she possessed. We will, of course, never know for sure, but she led her life nurturing and caring for her family and putting their needs ahead of hers like so many women of her generation.

|CHAPTER 2|

College and Formative Years

After my 10th grade (also known as SSLC in India), I enrolled in the Hindu College at Machilipatnam for what would have been a two-year Intermediate programme offering English, which was also the medium of instruction. Telugu was a second language, and optional subjects of specialisation were Biology, Physics, and Chemistry. I say "would have been" because halfway through year 1, my father was transferred to Nellore. Usually, a student was not permitted to leave in the middle of the academic year as there was no mechanism by which one could transfer credits in India. However, since my father was a senior officer in the Education Department and more so since he was transferred and backed up by my academic record, which was good at that time, a transfer was approved. I soon enrolled in the V.R. College in Nellore, which was an excellent college where the faculty was of a high calibre, the teaching was of a high standard, and the academic life was rigorous and well-rounded. The students I was surrounded by were there to absorb as much as possible and were generally curious and motivated.

I was able to integrate and settle into the new environment with ease. Although all the faculties were good, I would like to mention two of them. Professor Sachithanandam Pillai, principal of the college, was an outstanding English teacher. He taught us Shakespeare's "The Merchant of Venice". To my utter astonishment, he rarely had to glance at the book and knew most of the play by heart! He was clearly a lover of Shakespeare and his works, and he would not just read the play aloud but also break into enacting it and becoming the characters in it! This inspired a sense of awe and curiosity in us, and I have no doubt it was during those weeks and months that my own love of literature and Shakespeare blossomed!

In my later years, I would visit the beautiful and picturesque town of Stratford-upon-Avon, walk the same streets that Shakespeare supposedly set foot on centuries ago, and visit the cottage where he was born and which was the home of Anne Hathaway. I would also go on to watch many plays performed by world-class actors at the beautiful theatre in Stratford and the Globe Theatre in London, amongst other places. Most of all, I would myself go on to become a teacher of English literature and be able to rattle off long sections of Shakespeare's plays without needing to open the book!

Literature, and Shakespeare in particular, would go on to be not only a source from which I derived joy, fascination and a sense of wonder but also a vehicle that allowed me to relate to people in a different time, place and cultural context, some real and some imagined! It taught me early on about the diversity and evolving nature of the human experience and the similarities one could find with the people or characters in those books. I was also reminded about the timeless nature of things such as love, heartbreak, friendship, loyalty, greed, perseverance and redemption, which have changed little with the passage of time or the crossing of oceans.

And thus, a light was lit inside of me, the love of literature and the English language, that would burn brightly for decades to come, not dimmed one bit by the passage of time! For that, I will forever remember Prof. Pillai and be grateful to him.

Even as the love of the English language was taking hold within me and I was developing a deep-seated admiration for the beauty, nuance, wit and richness of so many famous literary works penned in England, some not that long ago and others centuries before, my mind could not help but think of the British people I had come across and crossed paths with in my own life when the flesh was not particularly warm or awe-inducing.

Whenever my father was transferred, as this was a regular occurrence, by virtue of him being a senior officer, his family, too, was entitled to travel in first class and needless to say, we, the children, looked forward to it! Every so often, a British officer would happen to be on the train we were booked on, and our first-class eligibility was at the mercy of the benevolence of the officer since he was entitled to occupy the entire compartment. On occasions, we would hear of Indian officers of my father's seniority having to travel 3rd class with first-class tickets. My father would have to appeal to the British officer to let us into the compartment as he was a govt. officer travelling on transfer. Most of the time, the British officer would "condescend" to let us in, but it was never a given, and we were always aware of this hierarchy that prevailed in almost every facet of life in India then. My elder brother, who could speak a bit of English, would sometimes go to the officer and speak a few sentences of English in a bid to impress him.

My own love of the English language remained intact and unaffected by my early and not-so-memorable experiences around those who played a part in bringing this language to India. In the following decades, I would go on to make numerous lifelong friendships and professional acquaintances in England that I cherish and treasure. Shakespeare, Hardy, Wordsworth, Blake and Keating transcended petty boundaries of nationality and race for millions of others who have not ceased to derive unbridled delight from their works. I went on to teach so many children, some of whom went on to become writers, teachers and literature scholars in their own right. And thus, I learnt early enough in life to never need validation or approval.

It is not as if my pursuit of English literature and the career to follow was inevitable. Long before I met Prof. Pillai, I had nurtured an ambition to study medicine and become a doctor. Whether or not it was a passing childhood phase that every child, for the most part, goes through or some long-held, deeply felt desire is not worth exploring in very much detail. I do remember my father told me that we would talk about my future studies once my university exams were over. I had a brilliant Chemistry teacher, Prof. David. Some of what he taught me still lingers in my memory to this day. My physics lecturer, Prof. B.P. Rao, was again someone who made a deep impression on me, and his lectures have stayed with me for decades.

In any case, my university exams were held in March of 1955, and the results were out in early June. I passed with good grades and duly started discussions with my father about what I should be pursuing. Though my grades would have given me a place in medical college, I fell short of the minimum age required by about two months. Interestingly, the District Educational Officer, who was none other than my father, was the competent authority to grant exemption in age in such marginal cases, but my father said that he would not use any special power to help his son. And thus, the medical college option was quickly ruled out. I, instead, opted for an Honours degree in English at the Andhra University, Visakhapatnam. My elder brother was already at the university studying Law, and I went with him. I found the location of the university extraordinarily beautiful, in the hills overlooking the sea. We could get a gorgeous view of the Bay of Bengal and its waves crashing onto the rocks from our lecture rooms and hostel rooms. It sometimes made me feel as if I was floating on the sea.

With College Roommates (From Left to Right) V.V. Subba Rao, M.V. Prasad, G.S.R. Sarma, V. Chiranjeevi (Andhra University, Visakhapatnam, 1957)

These years were consequential in helping me discover who I was, what drove me and what my unique talents were. They were not only a happy and carefree time but also a time of long discussions, fierce debates and intellectual arguments on every topic under the sun! They played a big part in making me more aware of my own strengths and weaknesses and, above all, instilling in me a sense of purpose for the years waiting for me.

|CHAPTER 3|

Krishnamurti and Rishi Valley

Annie Besant and her adopted son, J. Krishnamurti, founded the Rishi Valley School near Madanapalle in Andhra Pradesh. While working as a senior Education Officer in the region, my father had the opportunity to visit the school, and it immediately made a strong impression on him. I was then a student at Andhra University, and I recall his letter to me describing the school, the spacious 340-acre campus, as "unique and special ingredients that were hard to articulate in words."

The words written in that letter by my father would stay with me. After my post-graduation, I was considering various options I could pursue for a career, and as it happened, Rishi Valley posted in the paper an opening for an English teacher, and this caught my attention quickly. My father suggested I apply, which I did. I was promptly invited for an interview, and on my way there, I was fortunate to be able to attend Krishnamurti's public talk in Madras and even more fortunate to have a chance to meet with him.

He had an extraordinary presence and aura about him, and I was immediately drawn to him and what he had to say. "Krishnaji", as I would learn soon, was the name given to him by those who knew him well; he encouraged me to visit Rishi Valley and keep an open mind. At no stage did he suggest anything specific or advise me one way or the other. His detachment and lack of agenda intrigued me even more, and I was excited by the prospect of visiting Rishi Valley and finding out for myself what this "special ingredient" my father told me was all about.

J. Krishnamurti Gives a Talk at Rishi Valley, Andhra Pradesh, Circa, 1974

The principal of Rishi Valley, the eminent educationist Dr. Balasundaram, was also present in Madras for the talk. He said he was driving to the school the next morning and offered to give me a lift. This was another chance encounter that went on to have an outsized impact on me! I eagerly took up his offer and joined him on the drive to Rishi Valley. Along the way, he kept talking to me enthusiastically about Krishnaji, the school, and education in India. I was fascinated by his insights, and while he did most of the talking, I did chime in here and there with my own views, and I noticed that he would pause and listen to what I was saying and not in any way condescending or dismissive of someone decades his junior. This was the first of many wonderful conversations I would go on to have with Dr. Balasundaram, who, in my mind, was one of India's greatest leaders in school education.

The drive to Rishi Valley got greener and more picturesque as we got closer, and soon we were at "the mouth of the valley", from where the school was 2 km away. The landscape was dramatic – trees all around, hills on the horizon, the sound of birds chirping and gurgling streams of water. It was an expansive and spectacular setting for a school. Upon reaching the school, I was led into a room in the guest house. As it turned out, this was not to be a conventional job interview – I was requested to spend a week and get to know the school comprehensively! Dr. Balasundaram told me that over the course of that week, we would explore together if, from my vantage point, RV was the right place and, from his perspective, whether I would "fit in".

RV was a co-educational boarding school, and every staff member resided on campus. This was not surprising since the nearest town was a good distance away! Right from the beginning, I found it a voyage of discovery. I met most of the staff and senior students, sat in on classes, and observed the teaching of a few. I was struck by how informal the relationship between teachers and students was and the atmosphere of freedom that pervaded the place. The freedom did not manifest in chaos but was coupled with perfect order, and I remember noting how happy students and teachers looked! This happiness was not superficial or surface level but seemed to come from a place of deep love and a collective seeking of meaning in this institution of learning.

In the Rishi Valley Staff Room:
(From left) Dr. N.K.A Iyer, S.V. Venkatachalam,
S. Balasundaram and M.V. Prasad, 1969

The daily programme of the school included the usual academic work, sports, a variety of visual and performing arts and activities that enabled children to develop a love of nature and adventure, such as hiking and camping. The number of students in a class was between 20 and 25. Teachers welcomed questions, and for the first time, I was able to witness what an interactive learning environment looked like, where it was not always a one-way street from the teacher to the teacher but rather a shared journey of learning and discovery.

The hostels were called houses, and each house had a House Master or House Mother responsible for 20 or 25 students. Every teacher had to play a sport with students and coach them in the game if he/she was talented in it. The bond between the House Master/Mother and their students, who in many cases had come from homes and parents in geographically distant and diverse places, was clearly special.

And so, before I knew it, a week had gone by. The principal told me that they would be happy if I joined the school. I, too, felt a magnetic force pulling me to this "special place" that my father had written to me all those years ago. But, I decided to mull over the offer for a few days and told the principal that I would go back home, discuss the matter with my parents and then write to him.

I got back home and shared my impressions of the school with my parents. It was clear to them that I had found my calling, and they encouraged me by telling me to follow my heart. Thus, the decision was made, and I duly went on to inform Dr. Balasundram that I would be honoured to take up the offer to be an English teacher at Rishi Valley!

On reaching Rishi Valley, this time as an incoming young teacher, I was once again greeted by Dr. Balasundaram, who was his warm, reassuring and welcoming self. In addition to being an English teacher, I became a House Master and had to live with and look after around 20 senior boys.

When I actually started my work, I found it interesting and challenging. Though my M.A. was in English, I had no experience teaching the subject, so the principal suggested I work with Miss Hilda Yarrow, an experienced English teacher from England. Hilda was an excellent teacher who had a very unique way of conducting classes. She was a firm believer in interactive teaching and lively participation by students. Each teaching period was of a 40-minute duration, and Hilda blended in a variety of activities to prevent any monotony. She would read from the textbook, discuss what that passage conveyed, get the children to read aloud and write, and then ask them if they had any questions or needed clarification. Thus, every student was involved in whatever was being transacted in the class. Hilda was highly experienced and obviously older than me, but she was a humble, kind and friendly person who indulged me and mentored me as I was learning the ropes and finding my feet.

I found my students to be a delightful lot. I, too, did not take anything for granted and put in the work – I was invariably prepared for the class and always entered the classroom knowing that I had a duty to be open, available and compassionate to my students and that we were co-travellers in this journey of learning and discovery. As days passed, I felt myself slowly becoming part of the Rishi Valley culture and the students also seemed to be accepting me and we were developing a bond of trust. I found my work as House Master also interesting, even though there were occasions when I felt it was tiring.

Dr. Balasundaram and his wife, Mrs. Visalakshi, an outstanding Veena player of the old vintage, would invite me to their home, and we would have long conversations about various, sundry topics over dinner at their residence. Sometimes, before dinner, Mrs. Visalakshi would play the Veena, and we would be enthralled by her easy skill, obvious devotion and beautiful melody. She was an affectionate and loving soul, genuinely concerned about my welfare. She mothered me as if I were her child, and this helped me become part of the Rishi Valley culture and ethos even more. Dr. Balasundaram would ask me how things were, and I recall telling me how I enjoyed the teaching work and found it energizing. I felt a little exhausted by the House Master duties at times. His response was something along the lines of – "Prasad, boys will be boys, and at that age, they are passing through adolescence. We need to treat them with patience, empathy and firmness when needed. We should intelligently combine these. However, if you have any serious problems, please come and talk to me." The Balasundaram household was where I went not only for advice and counsel but also for good food, great company and unconditional love.

I spent time and invested in getting to know my students better – where they lived, what their parents did, how many siblings they had, how their pre-RV life was and what their dreams and aspirations were. Each had a unique story, and each had specific areas of strengths and blind spots/weaknesses, which had to be handled differently. While some of them needed to be constantly challenged with new goals, others had to be reminded that they needed to put in the long hours and hard work, while others still needed to be told not to derive their sense of worth from academic grades alone and that there was so much more to them than just their cumulative average of grades! I gradually began to understand what made each of them tick and what recipe was needed to get the best out of each of them, and I developed close bonds with all of them.

After a few months had passed, I began to slowly realize that the level of trust we had developed was, in fact, so deep that I could simply hand out a class test, leave the question paper and answer sheets with one of the students who would distribute them, collect them at the end of the stipulated time and pass them on to me. It was as if there was no need for me to be physically present in the classroom at all times and 'supervise' them! This gave me a great deal of pride, and I did not take this for granted, for I knew this was not the norm in most other places. While returning answer papers after grading, I would fold their answer papers and give them to each student individually. Thus, comparison was avoided. Krishnaji would often stress in his talks that comparison and competition were harmful.

Krishnaji emphasized treating each child like a beautiful flower and said that no two flowers were alike. Even in sports, gross competition was avoided; if someone played cricket, then they should be doing it for the love of the game with no pressure or with a narrow focus on the end result. Surprisingly enough, when a sport is played with a free mind, it, in turn, actually produces excellent results! The Rishi Valley cricket team would often play against teams from Bangalore. Two of our RV teachers were good cricketers from their college days, and they would coach and enthuse the students. Likewise, students played good tennis and other sports with the coaching and participation of talented teachers.

Not surprisingly, the standard of music and dance at RV was nothing short of outstanding, thanks in large part to Mrs. Balasundaram, who was a great musician and also a wonderful teacher. She also took great pride in working with the girls on dance, ably assisted by Miss Meenakshi, our Dance Teacher, who had received her training in the highly acclaimed Kalakshetra in Madras. Visalakshi produced some outstanding ballets under the magnificent open-air stage under the iconic banyan tree on the campus, and every ballet was a treat to watch. A new ballet production soon became a much-loved annual feature during Krishnaji's visit to RV. Krishnaji would sit with the junior children and enjoy it immensely. The students thus had a number of creative pursuits, and the cultural endeavour of the school complemented the academic work.

Among the many daily activities, special mention must be made of "Astachal". After all classes, as well as sports and extra-curricular activities had concluded for the day, students would have time to get refreshed and change. A bell would then go off for "Astachal," whose time was adjusted every few days to coincide with sunset and all staff and students would assemble on a nearby hill and sit in quiet contemplation for 6 to 7 minutes, and a sense of peace would prevail as we would all watch the setting sun go down behind hills and reflect on the day that had just gone by. Decades later, those moments spent watching the changing hues of the sky, young and old alike, watching the magnificent scene in perfect silence, feeling a shared connection with each other, with nature and our inner selves, remain firmly etched in my memory.

SECTION II:

People

|CHAPTER 4|
My Students – Part I

Early in my career, I became aware of the huge responsibility we carry as teachers in dealing with the future citizens of our world. While a good teacher can do wonders for a child's sense of what they are capable of and can inspire them to learn and achieve great things, a bad teacher, on the other hand, can dent a child's confidence and have a detrimental impact on their learning and growth. Thus, I was determined to give it all I had, be humble, become a continuous and lifelong learner myself, and always work towards being a better teacher each day, being open to feedback from my peers, superiors and students. It also meant being meticulously prepared for every class, which meant putting in multiple hours of work to enable an hour of teaching. And finally, it meant ensuring that every child was learning adequately and to the best of their ability – which invariably meant doing more than just grading assignments and handing out percentages. I would track the trajectory of learning for everyone, knowing that it could be different for each student, and the goal was to ensure everyone was learning optimally, even if not uniformly, at all times.

I took my role as a teacher seriously, but I did not take myself as a person too seriously! That meant we could share banter with the students, be open and vulnerable if I did not know the answer to every question I was asked, and most of all, be authentic at all times. My students, at all times, knew where they stood, what I expected of them and what they, in turn, could expect from me. This, I felt, was the bedrock of building a culture of excellence and a shared commitment to a journey of learning and growth.

I soon discovered something I found mildly surprising at that time but less so now as I look back – that this journey of growth was not one way by any means! Great students indeed bring out the best from a teacher. They have the ability to inspire and ask more of the person they are engaged in the learning process with. I was very fortunate to have taught some outstanding students early on in my teaching career. While I hope our interactions allowed them to be the best versions of themselves they could be, I am left with no doubt that I would not be the teacher I became without those shared experiences, discussions and engagement.

There were some extraordinarily gifted students, and I would sometimes go out of the way and spend extended time with them outside class hours to ensure they were sufficiently challenged and that I was setting the right expectations since they were capable of so much. I always believed that with great talent came awesome responsibility! I would not want anyone to be complacent or arrogant with the gifts they were born with but rather for them to set even higher learning goals for themselves and then attain those!

On the flip side, inevitably, there were also students who were less "gifted" in the traditional sense in terms of academics, and they would meet me after class for extra attention. What I would emphasise always was that every child was unique, and rather than lament about the fact that natural flair or what is referred to as "talent" in academics was not distributed by our maker in equal measure to every student, they should make the most of the qualities they did possess and work on opportunities to better themselves with preparation and practice. Also, one might be special in dramatics, pottery, poetry, sports or human relations. One just had to find who he/she was and embrace his/her strengths and weaknesses alike with humility and a healthy work ethic.

To help explore and widen the realm of possibilities, we started a Poetry Club, which would meet at regular intervals to listen to poems written by students and interested staff. Some students were so talented that some of their poems were published in Children's Poetry books. I wish to make a special mention of Listeners' Club, which would meet on Sunday mornings when interested students would quietly listen to tapes of classical music, Indian and Western. As a result of this, quite a few students developed an abiding interest in music.

There were a few "problems" too with children from super-rich families where they were provided luxuries and had an aversion to work, like making their beds and keeping their cupboards neat. Initially, they resisted that type of work though the other inmates were doing it happily. I had to counsel them and be tactful, patient and firm. Soon, they would fall in line. Not infrequently, I suddenly ran into one of my "boys" at an airport in places like Bombay, Bangalore, Delhi, London, Chicago, etc. He told me something like—"Sir, I am grateful for all that you have taught me at school, in the class and in the House." I think that is the greatest reward of being a teacher.

That was also the time when the Government of India launched a scheme of merit-cum-means scholarships in residential schools, and naturally, all the public schools, being residential, were included in the scheme. A few very bright children, most of them from vernacular medium schools, would join the school in Class 6 or 7. As Head of the English Department, I was given the challenge of working out a remedial programme to enable children to learn the required language skills in a year's time and join the "mainstream", as it were.

The scholarship students would be expected to attend all classes on the schedule, though to start with, they understood little of what was being taught. I developed a Remedial programme to fit their needs, and the English teachers worked hard with the group to bring them to the level of their peers in the class. We found the results encouraging and went on refining it year after year. The whole effort was so gratifying that most of them did very well in English at the Board exam. In fact, one of the students pursued English Literature at the college level, went to the US for higher studies and is now teaching English at a university there. When I recall the day she joined Rishi Valley, knowing only her language and seeing her today, it is amazing and gratifying. Another case is a boy who came with no knowledge of English and learned spoken and written English so well that he was the top scorer in English at the Board exam. He became a doctor in Eastern India. Many other scholarship holders went to IITs and found their way to Silicon Valley in California.

Rishi Valley School Staff, 1976

Some anecdotes and interactions remain in my memory. Like this boy who asked me this question in front of the whole class way back in 1963: "Sir, we are told that television will become a reality soon. I wonder if it could ever become possible for us to see the person while talking on the telephone." Most of the students looked amazed and a little amused by the question. My response was: "What a wonderful question! I won't rule out the possibility in future at the rate science is advancing." The student who asked me that question eventually went to an IIT after school and then to the US, where he took his PhD.

Then there was the boy in RV who had a rich vocabulary and felicity of expression. He could use words like 'iconoclastic' at the age of 13. I had been their English teacher and never encouraged my students to be bombastic. He knew both the meaning and usage of the words he was employing. He was a voracious reader and with a fine taste for books. Then there was the student who was excellent in English, went on to specialise in English at university and finally became a Foreign Service Officer. She distinguished herself in English in addition to classical dance. After an outstanding university education, she went to the US for further studies, became a professor of English at a leading university, and continues giving dance performances.

I remember the boy who showed promise as a stage actor and had the opportunity to act in school plays and later studied drama at the college level. He is now a renowned stage actor and director. Then there was the precocious child who wanted to read the "Time" magazine when he was just

10! He would come to our house in the evening and read "Time" and "The Hindu". Sometimes, I would quiz him about what he was reading and discovered, much to my surprise, that he not only understood what he was reading but could also discuss national and international affairs. I would quietly provide him with journals and books of a slightly advanced level to spur him to discover and stretch himself more. He went off to university and has since become a renowned Brand Specialist.

Another of my students got a scholarship from a top US university after school. After specialising in Biological Sciences, he returned to India, joined a top science institute and pursued his research and teaching. He received many prestigious awards and is today rated the topmost Biologist in India. I also remember the student who showed interest in Mathematics and Biology, which was considered a rare combination in those years. After school and IIT, he went to the US, where he studied and did research in Mathematics and Biology, eventually becoming a Computational Biologist, which he taught at university. He later returned to India and is now recognised as a top professor in the field.

I also had quite a few students in all my schools who would stand for what is right and never swerve from the straight path. I appreciated in private their steadfast adherence to values. I was fortunate to have a number of students who were brilliant academically, excelled in sports and other activities and exhibited character. They inspired me and made me feel that it is indeed worth being a teacher.

I learned at Rishi Valley that a teacher is constantly learning while teaching and that he/she should bring a fresh approach to the class and share new insights. The teacher has to be patient, humane, humble and firm when needed. The crux of the educational process is fostering the right relationship with students and always having their welfare at heart. If the teacher is positive and sincere, the boys and girls will invariably respond and feel secure. And above all, children should be happy as being happy is the beginning of learning, as Krishnaji reminds us.

I thus spent 19 rewarding years at Rishi Valley, which laid the foundation for me as a teacher. I was also uniquely blessed with many opportunities to interact with Krishnaji at Rishi Valley and at Brockwood Park School in England. Some of the teachers' meetings were intense, dealing with various aspects of the work of the teachers and the purpose of the K schools. In addition to the talks and meetings at Rishi Valley, I attended the public talks of Krishnaji at Madras, Bombay, Bangalore and Delhi.

In retrospect, I feel that the 19 years I spent at Rishi Valley has been the most enriching part of my life.

| CHAPTER 5 |

My Students – Part II

In my years of teaching across three schools, I have had to navigate my way through a few challenging situations, and I not only had to be resourceful, thoughtful and creative to find solutions that kept the best interests of students at heart at all times but also be mindful of my responsibility to upholding a high standard of academic achievement and also a strong ethical code of conduct that the institutions I taught at endeavoured to foster.

Each challenge was a learning opportunity for me, as it was for the students. At RV, one parent came and met my principal and told him that he was concerned that his daughter was constantly lagging in her levels of learning in class 10 in the English subject. My principal asked for me to meet the parent in his office to discuss the matter. I was a fairly young teacher back then, and I immediately told him that his daughter lacked interest in the subject, and that was the primary reason for her continued weakness in learning. The father simply said, "Sir, with all due respect, if a student hasn't learnt, the teacher hasn't taught." I was stunned by this statement and did not know how to react. My principal sensed the awkwardness in the air and quickly intervened and said, "Mr. R, please don't worry. Prasad is a good teacher keenly interested in his students. He will do some remedial English outside the class and ensure that she improves. Remedial

English is his specialization, too." Looking relieved, the parent thanked us and left.

That evening, I went alone for a long walk, thinking about what the parent had told me. Initially, I felt hurt, and my reflex was to be defensive and find fault with the student. Surely, it was not my fault if others in the class were doing very well in my subject, I told myself. But as I thought over the statement that he had made, "If a student hasn't learned, the teacher hasn't taught", more and more, I began to see the profound truth of what he had said. With this clarity in me, I walked back, feeling light and as if a burden had suddenly lifted! I decided to pour everything I could offer into the student. I regularly began to spend extra time with her after class hours, and soon enough, she began improving and caught up with the rest of the class, all in about a month!

There was another student who was widely perceived by almost every teacher of his to have a behaviour problem, and many of my colleagues felt that he should be sent home given the pattern of his disregard for the rules and standards of the school. Some of them spoke to the principal and me because I was the House Master of the boy. I, too, felt the student had a disruptive side to him, but I thought it would be a little unfair to write him off and send him home. This would crush him and his parents, and I did not want to recommend this. I, thus, took this up as a challenge. I was friendly and, at the same time, firm with him and counselled him patiently. I realized that what he really needed was more 1:1 attention, and he was yearning to be shown just a little affection and sensitivity.

We usually had a staff meeting on Wednesday evening where all the teachers would be present. The principal came to know that all his teachers, except me, would raise the issue of this boy being "a problem student" at the meeting. The principal, as it turns out, was himself not overly happy about the prospect of having to send a student home. I met him shortly before the meeting and told him I wanted the boy to be given a last chance. Looking relieved, he asked me to speak on those lines at the meeting. Expectedly, the concerned teachers raised the matter, and they wanted the boy to be sent home, though he was in class 12 and the Board exam was six months away. They all said he was incorrigible.

The principal then asked me how I felt on this matter since I was his English Teacher and House Master. At the expense of incurring the displeasure of my colleagues, I said that while he was a problem at times, I recommended we try and work closely with the student and not take the drastic last step yet. I suggested that we try to deal with him with firmness, patience, and compassion. I was not ready to give up yet, I vowed. My colleagues were surprised and felt a little "let down" even. The principal then asked me if I would stand surety for the boy. I readily agreed, especially since he was in class 12. The meeting then moved on to other items on the agenda. As we were walking to the dining hall after the meeting ended, a couple of my colleagues pulled me aside and said, "What has gone wrong with you, Prasad?" With more than a hint of sarcasm, they added, "We know you are a student reformer and want to be the saviour, but you have gone too far, dear friend." I smiled, and we moved on.

The principal impressed upon the boy the next morning that he was continuing in the school solely because of me and that he should positively change his behaviour from then on. The boy came to me with tears in his eyes and could not stop shedding tears. I consoled, motivated and encouraged him to study well and gave no room for any complaint from then on. He offered to give me that in writing; I told him that the teacher-student relationship was based on mutual trust and there was no need for written promises. We trusted each other implicitly. He was moved to hear that from me, and after thanking the principal and me and offering a solemn promise that he would change, he walked out slowly. I knew that was the beginning of the change in him, and soon all his teachers found a different boy in him – attentive in class, keen on learning, regular in submission of assignments and responsible in behaviour. Naturally, everyone was happy, and he left the school with good marks in the Board exam, which got him a place in a reputed college.

I was thus beginning to learn how to handle and change a "problem student". I realized with time that there were no problem students, but it was often we who made them problems through our lack of patience and understanding. Every student comes to school with unique talents and strengths, just as they do with blind spots and imperfections. The teacher has to bring the best out of the student, for which there is no single "right" way. The teacher has to be constantly learning, and only then will he/she be able to work with students and earn their confidence.

When I was a young, new teacher in Rishi Valley, I was also the House Master for senior boys. I was constantly mentored by my vice principal, who was my neighbour and also looked after another group of senior boys. Hardly two months had passed since I joined, and it was the time of Diwali, the festival of lights. It was a joyous occasion, and as is the tradition, all the staff and students would gather on the football field, light firecrackers for an appointed duration, return to their hostels, and retire to bed. One senior boy felt that for a new teacher, I was a little too strict. He hid a few crackers in his wardrobe and lit them next to my window at midnight. I knew something out of the ordinary was afoot, but I just pretended to continue to sleep. The vice principal woke up, came out and shouted, asking who it was, but the boys ran off to their beds before he came out. The next morning, I was perfectly normal and went to work as usual, which must have increased my feeling of guilt in him. He met me on the day of his return home and confessed to me with tears in his eyes that he was the one who planted the crackers next to my window. I still pretended that I was not aware of it. He held my hands and sought forgiveness. I simply brushed it off and told him not to let this weigh on him and that I had long moved on from this small act, carried out part in jest and part in ignorance. I learned through this incident that it is sometimes better to ignore acts carried out at the spur of the moment rather than glorifying them and giving the children a reaction that they are partly seeking momentarily. One cannot, of course, ignore the matter if it happens to be of a more serious nature or is carried out spitefully.

There was another interesting incident years later where the son of a senior minister broke some school rules and was on track to be sent home, in accordance with what his House Master and teachers recommended. I was then the principal of the school, and they spoke to the vice principal about it and stressed why it was important to take this decision urgently. I was always reluctant to send a student home until we exhausted every other avenue, and I was feeling uncomfortable about it. Just then, as providence would have it, his father came to our city on a work-related visit and was staying there for the night. My vice principal met him and explained the situation. The minister told him he would drop into the school the following day and meet me.

He duly came as promised and was profusely apologetic about what his son had done. I told the minister that while I, too, was not happy about sending the student home a mere three months before Board exams, my staff had given me their recommendation, and I could not ignore their opinion. In any case, we called the boy into my office, and his father told him, "Son, you have brought much discredit to me. You pack your books and clothes, as you will have to leave the school." The boy began weeping uncontrollably, and I had to step in and console him. I felt a deep sense of responsibility and empathy when the boy said, placing my hand on his head, "Sir, you are the only person who can save me." He promised me that we would find a big change in him if we gave him one final chance. I recalled how, decades earlier, I had helped turn around another boy in a similar situation in RV, and I could not bring myself to send this boy home. I thus relented and told the boy that he had to show me, his teachers, House Master and everyone else that he deserved this last chance. He did not let us down, and both he and his father were relieved and grateful.

After the incident, there was really a change in the boy; he began to take ownership of his own life and demonstrated an improvement in academics and his attitude toward his colleagues, teachers, and the school in general. He passed his Board exam with good grades.

Years later, I ran into him at Delhi airport, and he instantly came and hugged me. His father had passed away, and he had now become a minister and had come to Delhi for a meeting. I was extremely happy, and we chatted, reminiscing about his near expulsion, among other things. It was soon time for my flight. He invited me to his state, took my blessings, and we parted.

After all my years as a teacher and then principal, it is now my firm conviction that all children are born with varying levels of ability and talent. The duty of the teacher is to accept a child for what he/she is and not reject for what he/she is not. The teacher should know what every child is endowed with and start from there. Through observation with an open mind, hope, empathy and a positive approach, every child should be helped to reach his/her optimum potential. This inevitably varies with every child, and the teacher should never get into the vicious and escapist game of comparison, which can be devastating for a child. Every child has the ability to grow, learn and improve, and it is incumbent upon us as teachers to constantly evolve, adapt and find ways of enabling that in a creative, rewarding and positive environment. For this to happen, the teacher must be constantly learning, never be afraid to admit when they are wrong and have a deep sense of compassion and genuine love for children. These are the values and lessons that served me well during my time as a teacher, administrator and leader of schools.

|CHAPTER 6|

Towards Leading People

As I look back and reflect, I am increasingly of the opinion that my leadership learning started when I was a House Master at Rishi Valley. The House (hostel) that I managed had children, each coming from a different background and family situation but also possessing their own unique gifts and inevitably, each had their share of specific problems. When the students first joined the school, they were often homesick and needed attention, and I had to spend considerable time with them. Slowly, they would involve themselves in the daily programme and thus slowly come out of homesickness. Some of these very students would then go on to love school and hostel life so much that when it was time to leave school finally, they would only leave reluctantly. As House Master, I would do everything possible to help the students get involved in academic work, music, sports and activity/activities of their choice like visual/performing arts, debating, public speaking, creative writing, general knowledge quizzes, and science projects, amongst others.

It is not uncommon to have students from broken homes in boarding schools. To connect with and establish a level of trust and bond with them, as House Master, I would take extra care and try my best to create a feeling of security in them. The House Master, in many ways, acts as the Father, Mother, Counsellor, Friend, Philosopher and Guide to the students. From giving them a role in a play to providing them a chance to be in the debating team or encouraging them to play a sport of choice – there was not a set piece formula that worked with every child! One had to find each child's unique talent, passion, creativity and desire and then, after ascertaining the student had a basic level of aptitude for it, give him the opportunity to take up an extra responsibility. A few students could be helped this way, but many others would get involved in the daily routine/rhythms of a boarding school, organically strike friendships with peers and get on. As Krishnamurti said, "Being happy is the beginning of learning," in Rishi Valley, we firmly believe that a child must feel secure and happy.

There was an interesting boy in my House who hailed from South India. His father was a social activist who would go out of his way to help people who came to him, whether it was administrative help they needed from the local government or something else. G, as I recall vividly, was argumentative by nature and asked why he had to do whatever he was told or expected to do in a boarding school setting – from attending classes in a timely manner to everything else. But, once someone indulged him and explained why and helped him to see the point, he would accept his responsibility and not argue any more. On the other hand, if someone talked down to him and handed down an edict, he would not simply do as told! I was just a young teacher at that time, and his House Master found him to be a real challenge. I took the boy under my wing a little and made the extra effort to explain to him that if he was not punctual, he would make others wait, which is nothing short of a lack of consideration. Soon enough, he came around to think that I was being reasonable after all and that perhaps was the beginning of his trust in me.

That, in turn, was the beginning of a beautiful relationship between us based on mutual trust. We would sometimes go for long walks during the weekend and talk about a multitude of different topics. He was motivated by social justice, read a lot of history and believed that working people at all levels needed to be looked after — from the ordinary worker all the way to the Director. His sense of empathy, fairness, and justice appealed to me, and we often talked about them in our free time. He also was an excellent football and cricket player. I would share with him stories about great football players of that generation, such as Pele of Brazil, and cricketers of our time, such as Lala Amarnath and the great C K Nayudu, to name just two. Of course, it was not smooth sailing all the time, but this boy no longer was anything close to a "trouble-maker," as some of his colleagues were beginning to think just a few weeks earlier. Thus, I learnt a valuable lesson early on in my career — once a student is convinced that the teacher bore no malice, problems take somewhat of a backseat and mutual trust grows.

As my journey as a teacher and House Master continued to evolve and as I gained experience and confidence in my purpose, my principal began reaching out to me quite regularly, and we would have meetings where he would impress upon me that while continuing with my present work was critical, I should also take interest in new teachers, some of them beginners, and 'put them in the way' by talking about the way Rishi Valley functioned and pass along a list of lessons I had learned as a young teacher thus far. This was not indoctrination; rather, it was mentoring and was done in a friendly way without the feeling of mentor and mentee coming into it. Those interactions led to even greater clarity for me. It was quite a challenge to guide and help new teachers, all the while ensuring that I had to come across to them as their equal and with absolutely no trace of any hierarchy.

I was shortly thereafter appointed to be Head of the English Department and was given the task of coordinating work in the Department. That meant I had to acquaint myself with what was being taught in the senior section. As it so happened, there was already an excellent teacher from the US teaching English in the Junior Section and coordinating the work. I would, without being intrusive or disrespectful, do my own due diligence and check up on how my colleagues were getting on in their teaching or how they were grading written work, for instance, and when necessary, help them with some additional inputs and discussions. I would impress upon the teachers to go out of their way and explicitly note whether there was an improvement in the quality of work produced by a student after their correction or intervention. After all, that is the purpose of the "correction" we as teachers do – to enable and empower the students so that they can learn from their mistakes and show a path of improvement over time. On the other hand, if a student continued along the same trajectory and was repeating the same errors, it was our job as teachers to pay even greater attention to him/her, maybe even outside class hours if needed. Enabling every student to achieve their potential is our guiding goal at all times, and we must always find ways to achieve it! This process obviously differs from student to student.

(From Left) M.A. Hamid, M.V. Prasad, R.G. Mishra, Rishi Valley, Andhra Pradesh, 1977

I found fulfilment and joy while working with my colleagues, and I got the impression that most of them also had the same feeling as they were learning and growing as a result of our interactions. My principal, the great institutional leader that he was, would have informal meetings with me about my work. In hindsight, he was likely assessing my capability and suitability to take on more responsibility as a leader. The interactions with him, as well as my own experience and reflections, gradually led me to increasingly think about the importance of good leadership at all levels and, more pertinently, what made a leader good or not.

First and foremost, a leader is a part of a team and is often as good as the team around him/her. The popular belief is that a leader is always in the forefront and in the limelight, and this is often the case, but a good leader is also or especially one who never shies away from giving the members of his/her team a chance to drive the discussion or guide the collective towards the right direction! Rishi Valley is surrounded by hills and is an ideal place for going on hikes. It was the practice on Sundays for a teacher to climb a hill with a small group of students suitably accoutered for the small "adventure". The teacher would inform the principal and the dining hall in advance so they could prepare lunch packets. The group would leave in the morning and return by the evening. It so happened that on one of the hikes, owing to a miscalculation, we ran short of a lunch packet. I immediately offered to miss my lunch, but the boys would not agree to it; everyone in turn offered to miss him or share his packet with me, which was not acceptable to me. So, I used my seniority and insisted that I would be completely fine with a few biscuits and fruit we were also carrying. The students really appreciated this gesture, and they perhaps started respecting me a little bit more after this incident! Months had passed, but when a reference to leadership came up in a lesson, one student stood up and said in full earnest, "Sir, the character in the lesson reminds us of what you did when we went to climb Rishi Konda. As the leader, he serves himself last!"

On another slightly difficult hike with a different group, as we were returning late in the afternoon, we realised that we had lost our way. Some students became a little anxious and nervous as the day went on, but a couple of boys held their nerve, and we together could trace the right path. We returned safe, and this little adventure instilled in me and the students the importance of teamwork and not losing one's clarity and belief when the going becomes tough.

Working with colleagues of mine was a different type of challenge. One had to be friendly yet drive home the point in an effective manner. Young teachers often come up with new ideas and creative methods of their own, and they have to be rightfully encouraged to express themselves and try them. A leader needs to be patient, humble, and, most of all, have a healthy dose of empathy and good humour. He/she should be able to conduct meetings without the experienced members of the team feeling ignored or talked down to and yet, at the same time, enable younger teachers to feel valued and respected. I tried to keep an open mind, welcome new ideas, and discuss them with the team in a positive way. Ensuring the participation of all was paramount.

These experiences increased my self-confidence and laid the foundations in me even as they prepared me for what was to come — leadership in a school and educational context in a variety of roles, responsibilities, schools and places!

Launch of Book Edited Jointly with Mark Lee on Behalf of S. Balasundaram (From Left) Radhika Herzberger, S. Meenakshi, M.V. Prasad and R.E. Mark Lee, Vasanta Vihar, Chennai, 2012

|CHAPTER 7|
Mentors

As I look back, I feel fortunate to have met, interacted with and observed many great people, some closer than others. I have learned a great deal by closely watching how people react and lead when they are placed in various situations. Life has a way of throwing surprises at us, and nobody can claim to have mastered it all or to have a perfect answer to every problem they are confronted with every time! What is also true is that through a combination of observation, empathy, common sense and good old-fashioned practice, one can learn and become better with each passing year and handle situations that arise with grace, kindness, fairness, maturity, humility and courage. In particular, I would like to mention and talk about the influence that three mentors had on me.

My father, who was a senior Education Officer, maintained a room in our residence as his camp office. He would work from there sometimes and meet visitors too, some of whom were important officials or holders of public offices, such as the local Municipal Chairman, a Member of the State Legislative Assembly (MLA) or even, on occasion, the Member of Parliament (MP) of the parliamentary constituency. They would come to him on various occasions with requests such as transfer of officials, seeking bigger grants for certain schools or complaints about junior officers in the Education department. Sometimes, my father would ask me to sit in a corner and quietly observe. The visiting official usually did not mind the presence of an innocuous school or college student in a corner. These observation sessions helped me to learn a great deal just by listening to the conversations and marvelling at the way my father dealt with each of them. He was unfailingly courteous, would listen to them patiently and tell them that he had understood the issue and would follow up with the concerned section head and consider how best he could help within the framework of the rules he was bound by. He would assure them that he would be diligent in his follow-up, but he had, through his track record, also made it very clear that he would be fair – and sometimes that meant the officials would not quite get what they wanted!

The visitors would leave with a sense of satisfaction that my father had given them a patient hearing. He would follow up, gather the facts, calmly consider all aspects of the issue and take a decision. That's what a good leader should always do — listen patiently, be generous with time, display courteousness at all times, and, where needed, be tactful but always take the "right" decision later. As my father would often say, "If you do this, your conscience will be clear, and after a day's work, you will have a sound sleep." I slowly absorbed the import of these wise words.

On one occasion, I remember that an influential politician wanted him to make an adjudication that would have been against the rules. My father told him nicely but clearly, "I am afraid I won't be able to help you as I have a duty to abide by the rules." The leader tried to press his case, saying he could ask the minister to intervene in the matter. My father said politely, "Please request the minister to issue a letter asking me to do what you are asking." The visitor got the message and left the place without engaging further.

My second Guru was my principal at Rishi Valley, Dr. Balasundaram, who consciously built me up for a leadership role. As his headmaster, I had to frequently drop into his office, and he told me, "Please walk into my office even if there is a visitor, and if I felt on any occasion that I should be left alone, I will give you an indirect indication that we could meet a little later." But such occasions were rare, and he would normally introduce me to the visitor, and I would invariably join in on the discussion. These interactions were stimulating and served as wonderful lessons for a young teacher that I was at that time with a keen interest in children and also, as it would turn out, leadership in a school context.

I observed how Dr. Balasundaram would tackle difficult problems that were brought to him by our colleagues as if the problems were easy to solve. I also watched with admiration and awe as he dealt with political leaders at various levels, each with an outsized ego and an exalted opinion of themselves and the level of privilege and influence they were somehow entitled to! Often, various officials approached him for favours, sometimes sent by their political masters. He would be courteous but would seldom promise anything outside the norm, yet he had a way of reassuring them before he would send them away.

Once the visitors left, he would discuss the implications of the favours they had just asked for and how one should deal with the public courteously without the Head doing anything irregular. I would ask him questions, including hypothetical scenarios that came to my mind, and we would have a free discussion. He would often explain the pros and cons of each matter, and something he told me rings in my ears clearly to this day: "When you become an independent head of the institution, while in doubt, don't rush to arrive at a decision and repent at leisure. Stop the work, stay with the problem, let a night lapse and go back to it afresh the next day and you are likely to arrive at a satisfactory answer. Do not delay anything unduly, but be prompt in disposing of matters to your best satisfaction." This was not some bookish prescription that an academic dished out but was the wisdom of a man who had spent decades in the field painstakingly building an institution of excellence, a loving and thriving community of children, staff and parents around it and above all, a genuine interest in the welfare of the children who studied there. It would go on to serve me well in the decades to come.

He taught me so many things, and I would, in fact, say he taught me almost everything I needed to become a good leader. Etched in my memory are words such as: "When one is in a leadership position, never take a decision in haste, especially if you are disturbed. Wait for a while; that doesn't mean you are procrastinating! Wait for an hour or even a day, sleep on it if needed and be absolutely clear to yourself that you are making the right decision. Remember that good public relations are important but one can't set about pleasing everyone in the name of PR! PR is important, but only when it comes without sacrificing principles. Tact is important, but tact doesn't mean we twist facts. A leader's ingenuity lies in being nice to people without engaging in any irregularity. Insist on a culture of excellence and one where results are valued but never at the expense of principles. You will come up with your own techniques for managing people and institutions as you go along – remember to always work with colleagues as a team and keep your eyes and ears open!"

Besides discussions, advice and wisdom I so generously received from Dr. Balasundaram, I also had the good fortune of learning from people I met through chance encounters and real-world experiences during those years. I once took a group of Rishi Valley students to the Nilgiris on an excursion. Our programme included spending a few hours at the famous Lawrence School, Lovedale, near Ooty. On the appointed day, when we reached there, the Deputy Head received us warmly, and I inquired if I could make a courtesy call to the Headmaster, Mr. Thomas, the legendary Head. The Deputy told me I could knock on his office door and enter. When I did so, I saw Mr. Thomas busy grading his students' work. I introduced myself, and he was warm and courteous. When I said that I was an English Teacher and had heard a great deal about him, he said, "That's fine, Prasad; please note that you will pick up experience and become a Head eventually. I have two suggestions – please continue with your teaching. You may teach the final class, but please always find time to grade their written work yourself and promptly. Never go to your class and say that you couldn't grade their work or that you would return them the following day. If you ever do that, you will go down in their estimation. Taking the time to grade their work promptly conveys to them that you care! Let's not hide behind excuses and say one is too busy for these small but significant parts of being a teacher. Time is always there for a person who plans his priorities." I thanked him profusely for his time and the generosity with which he received a young teacher like me. I left my heart full of gratitude and a dose of inspiration that stayed with me long after we left Ooty. I learned a vital point from him and would always make the time to teach students as Head of School. And needless to say,

I would always grade my students' work promptly, no matter how busy I was!

Parents and teachers, especially in a residential public school setting, often get to know each other intimately as the House Master is often the substitute parent in a way when the child is in school. I was fortunate to come into close personal contact with a parent who was a businessman based in Calcutta and Madras. Mr. S.V. Narasimhan, or Mr. N as I will refer to him, hailed from Kerala, owned factories and ran a trading business. He admitted his son to RV, and the boy ended up in my House, under my charge, so to speak. Mr. N and I immediately developed a rapport and, in time, great regard for each other, and he went on to invite me to stay with him during one of my visits. Understandably, he was a very busy person with a calendar full of various matters needing his time and attention. But, he went out of his way and made time to sit down, interact and discuss various matters, some general and others personal, with me, including the growth and development of his children and the hopes and dreams he had for them. He was an enlightened, well-travelled and experienced man, and I benefited immensely from our interactions. I would often sit in a corner of his office room and observe how he was dealing with people and problems. Just as I had learned from my father and Dr. Balasundaram, I learned once again from Mr. N, although in a slightly different context, how a leader must treat his colleagues with trust, firmness and compassion. His business was one of the most successful, and he was known to almost all business leaders who treated him with respect.

With S.V. Narasimhan, Longtime Mentor, Chennai, 1983

One of his senior managers passed away, and the man, who was barely in his early forties, left behind a young family, his wife and an eight-year-old son. Mrs. N looked after the family for a full week, and the wife was offered a job in Mr. N's company and transferred to Madras, where the family hailed from. I was not in Calcutta or Madras at that time, but I learned about this from his son, my student. When I met Mr. N after a few months, he told me, "There was nothing extraordinary in it. I came up the hard way myself and can imagine how a family would feel if the breadwinner passes away. The position and wealth I have is not really mine. I am a trustee of all that I have and I would like to help others in need to the extent possible. And remember, there is no place for publicity in acts like that. It must be done quietly. As a trustee, I am expected to give back to society whatever is possible. In Sanskrit, it is called GUPT." In my interactions with him, I could make out that he helped many people –

poor, needy, students and others. I learned from him that leadership must be humane.

As I reflect and give thanks for the influence these great leaders had on me, I am particularly moved to this day when I think of the time that my father had a stroke and had to be hospitalised. All of his children, including me, took leave and gathered at Guntur, where he lived. We all took turns attending to him and staying by his side in the hospital. After a week, it became necessary for me to go back to Baroda, my place of work, attend to an urgent assignment briefly, and thereafter make a two-week trip to England that had been planned for months in advance. I discussed the matter with the senior physician attending to him. The doctor thought I could safely be away for 2 or 3 weeks. I explained to my father that I had to go to Baroda, clear the payroll, and sign cheques so that staff could get paid on time on the first of the month. My father's words to me were: "Prasad, duty comes first. Please go. Anyhow, the rest of the family will take care of me." I took his blessings and left. Sadly, he passed away 6 days into my visit to England. I rushed back by the first flight to be with my mother and the rest of the family, but it was, of course, too late to have a last glimpse of him. The man, my role model and hero, who taught me so much by example over the decades, uttered these as his final advice to me — "Duty comes first." These words ring in my ears constantly. To me, it was a great lesson that I have never forgotten and always attempted to live by.

SECTION III

Consequential Years Building Institutions

|CHAPTER 8|

New Paths, New Opportunities!

After 19 memorable, fulfilling and wonderful years in Rishi Valley, I made the difficult decision to leave and pursue new challenges. One part of me wanted the Rishi Valley life to continue forever, but another part told me that I had to find a new context after a long and consequential run in one place. Everything I knew about life, children, school education and administration had been in this unique and soulful place. However, I knew this was the time to set forth on the next adventure and find a new set of co-travellers and a fresh set of lessons to learn and share!

And so, I moved to Bhavan's Public School, Baroda, as principal, largely because of the persuasion of a mentor of mine, M.P. Chhaya, who told me more than once when I was at Rishi Valley that it was time for me to become an independent Head of a public school. Shortly after joining the school, I went around the campus and met students and teachers. It was immediately apparent to me that they were awaiting guidance and inspiration from the new head. Soon after, I held a full staff meeting, introduced myself and put forth my personal values, guiding principles and some broad themes of what I would look to do in the days and months ahead. Most importantly, I told them I would begin by listening! I started off by meeting the senior section students in small groups just to break the ice. I also had long meetings with the vice principal and the bursar to learn more about what was working, what was not and where they thought our focus needed to be in the short and medium term. One could almost instantly get a sense of the problems the school was facing – mainly, the place was hungry for direction and leadership, and the entire community of teachers, students and parents were patiently waiting for the new principal to settle in and begin to lead the place and hopefully help foster a sense of stability, purpose and clarity.

Dr. Chhaya Welcomes Prasad to the Bhavan's in Baroda. (From Left): Mrs. Bakshi, Mrs. Vyas, Mrs. M.P. Sheela Prasad, M.V. Prasad, N.S. Vyas, H.M. Bakshi, Dr. M.P. Chhaya, 1979

Bhavan's Baroda was a partly boarding and day boarding school and, at that time, only catered to boys. That was the first change that was already in flight as even before accepting the assignment, I had told my Board that I planned to make the school co-educational, and soon after, we admitted our first set of girls; it was a historic change that was a long time coming! We started small, with just half a dozen girls, mostly daughters of resident teachers. Sheela, of course, had played a big part behind the scenes in this change. One of the first girls admitted to Bhavan's Baroda was our daughter, Priya. The move was welcomed and embraced by all, and given how well things went, sure enough, the following year, we had many more applications for girls, and so pretty quickly, the co-education arrangement caught on! I was relieved and happy coming from a Krishnamurti school; education had to be co-educational, just as our wider world was!

Sheela and I felt relieved that the community had accepted us even though we were from outside Gujarat. Meanwhile, my team of advisors, comprising a few senior teachers besides the vice principal and bursar, and I had planned a fairly ambitious programme of action to tackle issues one by one. One of the first problems we tackled was that of "coaching". I found it jarring and unacceptable that students who needed additional academic help were being given what was called "coaching" in the school during what was earmarked as sports time. This "coaching" entailed the parents paying additional money! I met with a group of experienced teachers at the school, and we had an open discussion on the issue. Some of them also felt it was not really a desirable practice but had not questioned it before as they thought it was a "tradition" and did not want to ruffle feathers. Some others said that if the school did not arrange coaching, the day boarders would end up going to teachers' homes for tuition. This was a valid concern, so I listened to their views and asked them to think of a better way of helping low achievers, boarders, or day boarders and see if we could find a creative solution to the problem. We agreed to meet again two days later. So, we met again as planned, and I listened carefully to their ideas, and I put forth my own thoughts on the matter, and we agreed on "our plan". We agreed that we would identify students in need of extra attention through a diagnostic test. Once we knew the needs of each student, we would tailor a "remedial" programme and teach the students outside of normal class time. That way, the remedial programme would be need-based and time-bound. The teachers, too, responded well, and the programme started with the diagnostic test a week later. In short order, the teachers were ready with individually tailored plans for each student needing remedial instruction. Our new plan was thus accepted by all concerned, and we would hold review meetings periodically to iron out any glitches that came up. It was an early success, and we ensured that everyone got a say in the matter and felt like their voice mattered. We followed up and launched initiatives such as regular group meetings of teachers, subject-wise, and I would make it a point to find time to attend as many of these.

Addressing the School Assembly at Bhavan's, Baroda, circa 1982

Next on our to-do list was to improve what children learnt both in the class and outside the classroom. Through some friends and well-wishers of the school, we established contacts with the School of Education at the MS University in Baroda – a department that enjoyed a great reputation. We invited some of the faculty to meet our teachers we brainstormed on ways to systemically and measurably improve teaching standards. We appointed part-time specialist coaches for various sports, and that created immense interest in students. We also invited a couple of eminent musicians from the Music College to meet our staff and students and give special attention to some of our promising students. We also organised concerts and dance performances by visiting artistes, including some that were enabled by SPICMACAY. One particular step that went a particularly long way in lifting standards and morale in equal part was the arrival of the outstanding music teacher from Welham Girls' School, VS Deshpande, as a guest teacher for a fortnight each year. Deshpande Sir, as we called him, inspired our music teachers to embrace new songs and ways of teaching even as he himself taught some classes. Students and teachers greatly enjoyed the new songs he introduced to us and the generally positive disposition he exuded and projected!

We started another initiative where two visitors from the UK, Peter Holloway, a specialist in drama and Allan Stacey, an accomplished creative writer, would stay with us for a term of three months each year, and we immediately saw that their contribution was significant! Their stay led to a palpable improvement in the standard of written and spoken English. Peter and Allan would sit in on classes and teach and help the teachers with their approaches. Peter produced and directed a few wonderful plays, and Allan helped with various initiatives to improve oral and written English. Slowly, some of these atomic steps started having an impact. We observed that the motivation levels and standards of students began to improve.

Through the good offices of a personal friend, Pandit Ravi Shankar, the renowned Sitar player of international repute, ended up performing a benefit concert at the school, and thanks to the funds he helped raise, we built a new Kindergarten Complex.

Welcoming Ravi Shankar with Mohan Hemmadi, Baroda, 1982

When Ravi Shankar visited Baroda two years after the concert, we invited him to see his "gift" to the school. He was so moved and impressed that he himself said that he would perform at another benefit concert after just a few months! These concerts had several intangible benefits both inside and outside the school, as we could build a new reputation for the school, and many more students got interested in music and dance.

Staff Photo with Ravi Shankar.
Seated (from left) M.V. Prasad, Ravi Shankar, Ustad Allah Rakha, Mohan Hemmadi, Baroda, 1982

An outstandingly talented teacher, N.S. Ganesh, would organise weekly listening sessions for interested students, aptly named "Raaga Maalika", where Ganesh would speak a few words about the song before playing the tape. These sessions were organised in the small hall on the ground floor of the principal's house and benefited about 20 students who were "regulars". The impact of the sessions can be gauged by the fact that some participants carried on their interest in music long after they had graduated from our school! One student even spent a year in Dharwar, the cradle of Hindustani music, as a disciple of the legendary Mallikarjun Mansur and learnt music. That student is now an acclaimed University Professor in Hyderabad, but his love for music remains, and he credits "Raaga Maalika" for this! It is gratifying to see the truth of the thinker who said that education is what remains in the individual after leaving school. This was a learning point for me – Real education, as they say, is an activity where both the teacher and the taught learn!

With Long-time Friend and Colleague, N.S. Ganesh, Baroda, circa 1986

Our school also hosted the National Council for Educational Research and Training (NCERT) sponsored music camp for music teachers of public schools from across the length and breadth of India. It was directed by the famous musician Kanu Ghosh. The programme comprised patriotic as well as socially themed songs from every major Indian language, and participants learnt these songs with great interest; they would go back to their respective institutions after the conclusion of the camp and, in turn, teach these songs to their students. Something as simple as that ended up serving as a very useful project for forging national integration! Teachers and children alike learn new songs in various languages, and to this day, many of them, including me, hum and sing these, like the haunting and melodious "Aye Maati Re" in Assamese or "Aata Uthavu Saare Raan" in Marathi, to name a couple.

In a bid to encourage students to communicate more with one another in English, Allan Stacey introduced a small trophy called the "Peacock Award for Cultural Endeavour". The purpose was to encourage speaking English at school with no discouragement to speaking Indian languages. He was able to strike a fine balance between encouraging the use of English in the school, especially since we were an English medium school, and at the same time, carefully showing due respect to every Indian language, which went a long way in promoting an environment where children could grow up comfortable in their own skin even though they learnt the use of English in an increasingly globalised and international world.

Exposure to role models and people of repute to broaden the horizons of our children was another key initiative we took on. We invited eminent people to visit the school, such as Mother Theresa, Swami Shankaracharya of Kanchi, Swami Ranganathananda of Ramakrishna Mission, Dr. Kurian of the famed AMUL Dairy, Mrinalini Sarabhai, the noted dancer, Dada Vaswani, the well-known educationist, father Kunnunkal, who headed to CBSE and also cricketer Kiran More who was a regular visitor and also gave a few lessons to our school cricket team. Most of the visitors addressed groups of students and interacted with them. Father Kunnunkal, in fact, was so impressed with the school during his visit that he granted the school "Permanent Affiliation" at his address, which was rare! The parents were elated at this and the prestige of the school went up further.

I had a strong conviction, and this was strengthened during my time at Rishi Valley, that having eminent persons regularly visit the school greatly inspired growing children. It unleashed forces of imagination and possibilities in their minds, and this was something that had immeasurable value! And so, this tradition took hold and grew with time. A professor of English and a noted writer Birje-Patil, eminent dancer and Professor Chandrasekhar, the great musician Narayan Rao Patwardhan and a host of artists from the Faculty of Fine Arts at the University, in addition to many eminent academics, were frequent visitors. Professor Govinda of the Education Faculty, who later went on to become Director of NCERT, regularly interacted with teachers, much to their benefit. My friend, philosopher and guide, M.P. Chhaya, would often visit us from Delhi to meet teachers and students. He was a big help and inspiration to me and a genuine well-wisher of the school.

(From Left), C.V. Chandrashekhar, Mrs. Chandrashekhar, Padma Subramaniam, M.P. Sheela Prasad, A.B. Advani, M.V. Prasad, Bhavan's School, Baroda, 1984

We also placed a lot of emphasis on inculcating a strong belief in our children about the power of social work. Groups of students visited Mother Theresa's Home, spent time with the people there and donated clothes and food items. The Sister running the Home once told me in confidence that she saw a smile on the faces of the people and added that they often asked her when the students would come next! The students, too, developed an attachment and looked forward to their next visit. One sensitive girl movingly spoke about how she felt the presence of God in the smile of the people she interacted with at the Home.

Groups of Students from Bhavan's, Baroda Visit Mother Theresa's Home, Baroda, 1989

Staying with the theme of social work and the importance of sharing and giving, our students would hold a Fun Fair on the campus with senior students opening stalls and selling food items. Having a good time once in a while was completely fine, especially to blow off some steam during the busy months preceding the Board exams. But we talked about how to make a fun fair more meaningful – what if we donated profits from the fair to the Helpers' Welfare Fund? To the credit of the students, they received this suggestion with alacrity, and we formed a small group of students and teachers to organise the fair and collect contributions. The group would ultimately hand over the total profit received to the three senior most helpers in our office. As they handed over the proceeds, the faces of the students would say it all – a sense of joy and satisfaction at having helped someone in need! One of the main functions of the school is to help growing children become sensitive to the less fortunate and help them with no patronising airs; the amount, big or small, didn't matter; what mattered was the feeling behind the work. We were certain that they would continue to take part in such activities in their college career and beyond.

One of the main purposes of education is to inculcate values among children, and I was happy we could do a little work in this direction. As a school, if we could send out students into the wider world having developed some of these finer feelings that they could carry with them, we would have been successful! The school began to thrive, and we collectively were taking significant strides in providing quality all-round education to our children, and my own perspectives, as well as those of my colleagues, got sharper and developed in the process. The school had improved vastly, and so did I – both as an educator and as a person!

In 1993, when I was leaving the school after 14 beautiful and eventful years, the entire community – students, parents, the public, and my Board, who had always been supportive, was sad and tried to prevail upon me not to leave. That, to me, was a sign of the journey we had undertaken and the success we collectively achieved. That was the validation I needed! We said goodbye to all concerned and thanked them for a ride of a lifetime. They said I was leaving behind a much better school, but I felt within myself that the school had made me a better and more seasoned principal and, hopefully, a more wholesome human being.

Staff of the KG Section, (Seated from Left) Mrs. A.I. Singh, Miss K. Dhruva, M.P. Sheela Prasad, Mrs. Advani, Bhavan's School, Baroda, circa 1990

Graduation Ceremony for Outgoing 12th Standard Students, Bhavan's, Baroda, 1990

|CHAPTER 9|

Building and Re-Building!

Our time in Bhavan's Baroda was equally fulfilling, enjoyable, and eventful. Our children Priya and Srinadh had their formative years there. They grew up happily and began discovering the world amidst friendship, camaraderie and affection. Growing up as children of the principal had its privileges and challenges, too, and in their own way, they found a sense of who they truly were and charted their own unique identity, distinct enough from their parents. In her time in Baroda, Sheela, too, had made significant strides as a child education specialist and demonstrated at-scale approaches that made early childhood education happy, nurturing and supportive of learning for every child, no matter their specific gifts or challenges! And for me, these 14 years were transformative – they allowed me to become the Head of a school, embrace the challenges fully, develop my own methods of fostering excellence and finally, enabled me to make an impact on the people I crossed paths with in ways I could not have imagined as a young English teacher in Rishi Valley! It was a grand canvas, and I thoroughly relished painting on it, but change is inevitable, as they say, so the time came to bid goodbye to Bhavan's Baroda and embark on the next adventure in 1993.

My next destination was the Arabian Gulf, where I took over as Principal of the Indian School in Bahrain. It was a big change from the Bhavan, from Baroda and from India! But Sheela and I immersed ourselves in learning about the new place — what worked and what needed fixing even as we made new friends, got to know our colleagues and found our feet in a new context! Our two years in Bahrain gave us a new perspective on expatriate life as well as the unique aspirations and apprehensions of those who leave home to make a living abroad so that they can offer the best possible future for their children who are growing up in a unique cultural amalgamation as they straddle between India, the Gulf and more often than not, Europe, North America or Australia where many of them end up going for university education.

I soon found that academic standards were high in all Indian Schools in the Gulf. But the biggest challenges for us as administrators of a prestigious school were often outside the confines of the classroom and school campus – how could we, as administrators and teachers, help parents so that their children grew up without a sense of entitlement or confusion? Instead, how could we together summon the best of what their Indian upbringing and the possibilities of the Gulf offered so that we fostered secure and curious children who were comfortable with who they were and ready to travel and take on the world?

It was a great learning experience in the Gulf for me. But I felt that two years there was sufficient time, and I was ready and eager to return to India! As I surveyed the landscape and indicated my interest in returning home, I was glad to know that I had a few offers from public schools to choose from. After some thought and deliberation, I opted to go to The Daly

College, Indore. Daly was one of India's iconic public schools, along with Doon and Mayo, and the opportunity to serve there was just what Sheela and I were looking for at that stage of our careers and life. Sheela and I were no strangers to the school, as, just a few years earlier, we had marvelled at the campus when we attended the IPSC conference that took place in Indore. Little did we know at that time that we would return there one day to live and serve!

When Sheela and I reached Indore by train, we were pleasantly surprised to see the vice principal, head boy and head girl on the platform to welcome their new principal. We were then promptly escorted in a car to the campus, and instead of the majestic principal's bungalow that we were familiar with from our last visit, we were dropped off at another bungalow, certainly no match to the official bungalow! I learnt that the previous incumbent had not yet vacated the official residence. The school administration, of course, did their very best to make the other bungalow as comfortable and welcoming as possible, but one could sense the awkwardness in the air!

Soon after assuming charge, I had a meeting with the president and vice president of the Board of Governors. They were gracious and welcomed me wholeheartedly, and without wasting any time, candidly told me that the school was, in fact, facing a lot of problems lately, and they projected confidence in my ability to turn things around! I would quickly learn about the various problems the school was mired in. In fact, I learned that the teachers had recently been on strike to express their strong disapproval over my predecessor's sudden decision to rusticate several students of class 12, a mere 20 days before the final Board exam. They were asked to leave the hostels at once and come to school premises only to write their Board exams. The staff thought this was an unusually harsh decision, and that too at such an important time in the academic calendar. The principal refused to hear the concerns expressed by the teachers and stuck to his stand, which led to the unprecedented teachers' strike in support of the students. The Board subsequently terminated the Head, and he went on to file a court case against the Board for unjustified removal and refused to leave the bungalow till the case was decided! Court cases move slowly, so I knew that instead of dwelling on the unpleasantness surrounding the official residence, Sheela and I would have to get used to the interim accommodation and make it our home.

The next day, I met the students at the School Assembly and the teachers during the customary tea break. Not surprisingly, as I interacted with them, I found the children to be curious, inquisitive and hungering to communicate with the Head. The teachers, too, were enthusiastic and keen to teach, and they had nothing but the best interests of the institution and the children in mind. The Bursar, administrative staff and helpers seemed efficient and diligent. But I also very clearly saw how they all looked at me and spoke to me with high expectations of me! Later that evening, I shared my feelings with Sheela and told her I felt the weight of the expectations of so many, and we could not let them down. Sheela, as ever, showed great maturity and expressed every confidence that we would set things right. She also gave me some much-needed tactical advice and boosted my morale. Our work was cut out, and as for me, I had to do whatever I could, mustering every ounce of energy and drawing upon all the resources I had accumulated over the years to set this place right and restore normalcy, credibility and hope.

The Annual Prize Giving was fast approaching, and the vice principal had worked on the programme, which was almost ready, and rehearsals were in full swing. I sensed that this could be a pivotal moment to inject a sense of anticipation and hope that was badly needed by all! And so, we poured our energy into getting the details and the tone of the function just right. The big day came, and the attendees were happy with the programme; they particularly liked the Principal's Annual Report, which was not merely a drab recounting of the achievements of the year but carefully blended within it was my vision and hope for the future. I reminded everyone that Daly College had a rich and glorious history and so much to draw from. This was appreciated by all attendees, in particular, the Chief Guest of the function, who was the Chief Minister of the state and a distinguished alumnus of the school who made a reference to my speech in his address and expressed his earnest hope that the turnaround of the school was already in motion, thanks to someone nurtured in the "Rishi Valley culture" in his telling. In hindsight, this was a key turning point in the revival of DC.

Thereafter, the CM, Digvijaya Singh and I became close, and he was invariably helpful and supportive of the work we were doing. He was a partner and believer in the process we had set forth of listening to everyone, fostering a culture of teamwork and re-building trust to restore Daly College to its rightful place of being an institution of excellence.

The next critical test was the 12th class farewell function. This function had, in fact, led to major problems for the previous Head, and it was now just a few weeks away! Sheela and I brainstormed a novel approach, and we set forth to plan an entirely different way of conducting it. We called it the "Graduation Ceremony" and invited the parents of the graduating students to attend and join us for dinner, after which those who wanted could take their children home to prepare for the Board examinations. The function, in some ways, resembled a University graduation ceremony but was suitably adapted to a school context, and we blended in aspects of Indian tradition with beautifully curated songs with a theme relevant to taking leave of one's elders and friends. The attendees were left mesmerised and were deeply appreciative of the touching function. Many parents had travelled from far-off places and were thankful to the school for organising a graceful and touching farewell for their children. Students, staff, and board members alike felt that a sense of belonging was restored. I have always found it remarkable that the small details often determine how people perceive and remember a time in their lives! This function played an outsized role in restoring a sense that Daly College truly cared about its children, and this sense of hope and optimism persisted well after the melodies of the evening faded.

Graduation Ceremony for Outgoing 12th Standard students, Daly College, Indore, 1997

I also reminded myself that it was vitally important for the Head of the school to feel the pulse of the children without a lot of layers in the middle! I thus went on regular visits to the hostels, and Sheela and I interacted with boys and girls whenever possible. I would watch the students play sports and attend practice sessions for drama and musical programmes. I would also make it a point to interact with the teachers in charge of these activities and give my suggestions and observations. I was reminded that the essence of managing a school lay in bringing people together towards a common, shared goal! So, I strived to bring my colleagues and students together, discuss and brainstorm with them not only about issues but also invite their suggestions and, finally, accept all those that were relevant. Indeed, some of the best suggestions I heard came from the youngest in the room! This collaborative approach built a sense of trust, which is the only basis on which a school can be run. I was learning a lot through participative management.

Soon, it was time for the year-end Board examinations. That year, we took extra care of the preparation schedules, arranging extra help from the concerned teacher for the students who needed it. We also had individual meetings with every student to motivate and set goals for the students. I had group and individual meetings with the staff teaching the Board exam classes—again to motivate, encourage and guide them. The vice principal and heads of departments began working with renewed enthusiasm. On exam day, I would go into every classroom before the question papers were handed out and greet and bless the students in an effort to build their confidence. After that, I kept away from conducting the exam and met the students as they came out after the exam. I guided, advised, and encouraged them.

The Board exam results were very good, and many parents and students met with me for guidance about college admissions. I would take the time and give letters of recommendations for students trying to go abroad for higher studies. There again, I would guide them with university choices in the UK, USA, Australia and Canada and also connect them with alumni studying there.

The school already had a fine record of sport—it produced national-level and state-level cricket players. We made a concerted effort to improve the standards of various other academic and co-curricular activities, prompting one of the parents to say, "The school now aims to provide wholesome education". Gradually, the prestige of the school went up, and demand for admissions increased dramatically, which was always a sign of how well a school was faring! The international pursuits and connections detailed in previous chapters further strengthened the school.

Put together, one day and one student at a time, we changed the ethos and atmosphere of the school! It was not something any one person could do by themselves; it was a team effort! We at Daly College went from a sense of hopelessness and rancour to a thriving, collaborative and happy educational centre of excellence that re-discovered its greatness! Indeed, greatness is not measured by awards, buildings or endowments but by the daily work of creating joyful, thoughtful and innovative citizens of our world.

Book and CD Release of "Sing Along" by M.P. Sheela Prasad. (From Left) Mr. M.V. Prasad, Mrs. M.P. Sheela Prasad, Board President N.S. Bidwal, Chief Minister Digvijaya Singh, Daly College, Indore, circa 2000

|CHAPTER 10|

Public Schools!

I have been very active in the Indian Public Schools Conference (IPSC) since 1979, when I became a member. In fact, I got a taste of what the IPSC was about even before that when, as Headmaster of Rishi Valley, I attended an annual session of the IPSC at the Hyderabad Public School as my principal was abroad and asked me to stand in for him on behalf of the school. I had the opportunity to interact with and learn from other senior principals. When Rishi Valley hosted the Conference in January of 1979, G.N., the Principal, entrusted me with the job of pulling together the overall planning, logistics and organization of the entire conference as he would be tied up interacting with the various heads and taking the opportunity to speak to them at length about the teachings of Krishnamurti and the philosophy of Rishi Valley. A few senior heads, they told me later, noted the perfect arrangements made and marked me in their minds as a potential head in time to come. As luck would have it, just a few months later, I was invited to be the principal of Bhavan's Public School in Baroda, Gujarat.

Over the years, the annual IPSC conferences provided me with an intimate opportunity to observe, interact, and share the wisdom and advice of many great leaders. I especially learnt a great deal from veterans such as H.N. Kashyap, J.K. Kate, Shomie Das, Dr. S.D. Singh and B.K. Sood. They rose above their regular duties to their own institutions to spend their time and energy furthering the reputation and solving problems facing Indian Public Schools as a group, and that, to me, was laudable. Running a public school in the 1980s and 1990s was complicated. There were pulls and pressures from the governmental agencies, though the schools themselves did not receive any financial support from the government. The schools had to fight really hard to retain their independence even while not coming across as obstinate or elitist!

Over time, it also became somewhat of a fashion statement for political leaders of all stripes to rail against these schools in public, even though they secretly appreciated their standards and discipline. It was not surprising that quite a few of the very legislators and ministers sought admission for their own children in the same schools they were publicly calling out as out of touch and a relic of the past. The implication was, of course, that public schools were a vestige of the British Empire since some of these same institutions were founded during the British Raj and patronized by the children of the officers of the British in addition to royal families and other people who had the means.

Indian Public Schools over the years did see enlightened leaders such as Karan Singh, V.K. Krishna Menon, and the first Vice President, Dr. Radhakrishnan, take a stand and lend support to the cause of these schools, not just because some of them studied at these very schools but also because they recognized the role these schools played in preparing the leaders of tomorrow. They might have had their own misgivings about some aspects but concluded that the national discourse would be better served by taking along the views of public schools as opposed to treating them as "the other" and either ignoring them or unfairly categorizing them as not serving the common good.

As far as my own journey with the IPSC went, at a personal level, I earned the trust and confidence of one of the stalwarts, Mr. Sood, who went on to serve as the Chairman and he ultimately nominated me as the Secretary of IPSC and I learnt a great deal from him. Among the chief lessons I learnt were to strive to make the organization more inclusive and to discuss issues in the open. The reputation of the IPSC being a clique where opaque decisions were the norm had to be changed, and we were conscious in our efforts to do so! Mr. Sood also believed in continuously serving the cause of the IPSC and continuing to work towards various initiatives well into his retirement — to this day, he continues to play an active role in IPSC, which is remarkable and inspiring! He has been a member for many decades and rarely missed the annual conclave of principals. I went on to succeed him as the Chairman, and all that I had observed and learnt from him helped me immensely.

I also need to make a special mention of Dr. M.P. Chhaya, who served for many years at a famous public school and later moved to the Bharatiya Vidya Bhavan. It was he who was largely responsible for my moving to Baroda from Rishi Valley. Dr. Chhaya took me under his wing and was a mentor to me in my formative years as a young principal who was learning the nuances and complexities that came with the job. He also talked to me about the uniqueness of Bhavan's institutions and pitfalls I should be aware of and shared with me his toolbox, as it were, on how to respond to various situations one would inevitably face as Head of a school!

It is needless to say, this relationship and the support and advice I received from him went a long way. "Be positive always, Prasad! Try out new ideas responsibly; do not just sit in your office all day; be on the move and visible; enlist the participation of all staff by intelligently delegating work, and finally, do your own bit for the future by spotting and grooming the next generation of potential heads of school", were some of what I learnt from him. Those words still resonate with me, and I will never forget those pearls of wisdom. He would tackle the toughest of problems by listening to all parties calmly and patiently and, after a great deal of thought and deliberation, suggest a way forward impartially. Thus, everyone left satisfied with what he decided, even if they initially had misgivings, for he was always transparent, fair and generous with his time. His main principle was to move forth with hope and positivity. He was ready to back that vision up and put in any amount of work—his colleagues would say he believed in work, and that's what he did even from his sick bed before he breathed his last.

Another legendary figure in public school circles and school education, in general, was Shomie Das. He holds the distinction of leading three of the finest public schools in India — Mayo College in Ajmer, Lawrence School in Sanawar and, of course, Doon School in Dehradun. For a man of his stature and repute, he was remarkably approachable and easy to strike up a conversation with. When he did talk to you, you would get nothing but his complete attention — it did not matter if the person he was talking to was a student, colleague, parent or visitor. He had a magnetic personality and instantly won the confidence of every person he came in contact with.

Shomie Das and other legends who were his contemporaries of the time, namely, S.D. Singh of Scindia School in Gwalior and Peter Rogerson of Rajkumar College, Rajkot, contributed greatly to founding the IPSC Trust. The Trust would collect contributions from member schools and offer merit cum means scholarships to children whose parents could not afford the fees of member schools. This was a key reform that went a long way in making public schools more inclusive and accessible to those who were not born in wealth or privilege. This was something many in the IPSC circles wanted, but it was the untiring efforts of the aforementioned senior principals that finally took shape. To this day, the Trust continues to do this service and has been instrumental in helping educate some very bright minds who are doing very well in various walks of life in India and abroad. Thus, the Trust is not only doing noble work but also helping to partly erase the "image" that public schools are only for the affluent classes.

I also have to acknowledge the role and influence of another senior whom I worked with closely, a remarkable person, Mr. S. Ramakrishnan, Executive Secretary of the Bhavan. He had worked with India's preeminent leaders, such as Sardar Patel and K.M. Munshi. In fact, it was Mr. Munshi who founded the Bharatiya Vidya Bhavan, and he promptly appointed S.R. as the Executive Secretary. S.R. was unfailingly courteous, believed in and practised simple living, and always advocated a cautiously optimistic model of slow and steady growth over rapid expansion that did not pay attention to the feedback from all stakeholders of an institution. Unlike corporate companies, the goal of education institutions was not to deliver unfettered growth for the sake of it but to enable the citizens of tomorrow to imbibe the high ideals that the Bhavan stood for — all-round excellence, a grounding in the wisdom of our ancient culture and a respect for the communities we operated in and the people that we worked with — from the helper who kept the school premises clean to the most affluent parent!

With S. Ramakrishnan, Executive Secretary, Bharatiya Vidya Bhavan, Principal's Residence, Bhavan's School, Baroda, circa 1983

I had the opportunity to be the Principal of Bhavan's Public School, Baroda, for fourteen years. S.R. gave me all the support I needed to develop it as an excellent school, and once he felt confident that I understood the charter and ethos of the Bhavan, he gave me all the freedom I needed. He had his own way of assessing how the school was doing. He never failed to appreciate progress and positive growth while not hesitating to help me correct the course as needed! As a young principal, if I was unduly insistent at times, he would remind me with his characteristic smile about the virtue of taking everyone along in decisions of the school and to always remember that we all desired the same things albeit at a different pace or by taking a slightly different route to get there! I learnt much from his way of functioning. For instance, if someone was being unreasonable, he taught me the virtue of not reacting but remaining still. More often than not, the person would realize that they needed to change course, see reason, and often go on to express regret.

Being a prominent personality in educational and cultural circles, he had access to dignitaries like the President and Prime Minister. Sometimes, he would invite them to important functions at the Bhavan, and gradually, they would become a part of the Bhavan. He stayed away from politics but drew support from political leaders across the landscape for the institution. He even established Bhavan's centres in the UK and USA and called them Institutes of Indian Culture. These international centres are doing great work in teaching Sanskrit and Indian music and dance. I recall with fondness the time I spent with S.R. visiting the Bhavan in London and the many things I observed, admired and learnt from him. He was a larger-than-life figure whose greatness is in the legacy of the institutions he left behind, which continue to grow and thrive well after his departure from this world.

As I reflect upon my years in and around the IPSC, I cannot but be thankful to the many people who gave me their time, advice, counsel, life's learnings and generosity. In fact, those interactions and learnings helped me navigate the challenges of being a better Public School Head and reminded me to pass on my lessons learnt to the next generation of leaders, which I unfailingly went on to do!

SECTION IV

Passages from India to the World

|CHAPTER 11|
First Travels Overseas

Growing up as a young boy in various towns of Andhra Pradesh, my exposure to countries beyond India mostly came from books and literature. If someone had told me that becoming a school teacher would go on to pave the way for me to travel widely around the world and learn from and interact with top leaders in the field, I would scarcely have believed them! As it turned out, I had the good fortune of making numerous acquaintances during my travels abroad, many of whom taught me a great deal and went on to become friends for life. I also had the opportunity to compare and contrast the unique approaches, challenges and innovations in school education across the globe, and I was all the richer by these experiences!

Shortly after I became Headmaster of Rishi Valley in July 1974, my principal had the opportunity to address the British Council officers, and soon after that, I was asked to visit their office in Madras for a discussion. During our interactions, I told them I would be quite interested in visiting a few schools, both Public and State schools. I also told them about my long-held dream of someday having the opportunity to personally visit the places and settings connected with Thomas Hardy and Wordsworth, which I knew so much about through books! Visiting Stratford-upon-Avon, the birthplace of the great Shakespeare, would be the icing on the cake! And, of course, no visit to the UK would be complete without paying homage to the hallowed grounds of the various colleges of Oxford and Cambridge. The English Studies Officer was mildly amused and mightily impressed with my specific preferences and desires and promptly granted me a two-month "Visitorship" (somewhere between a paid sabbatical and an internship but for experienced English teachers). He carefully drew up a programme which included all my interests. And to top it all off, he told me that I would be attending a Summer School to teach English at Leeds University.

Upon reaching London on my maiden visit abroad, I stayed for three days with some friends before the official portion of my visit kicked off. I explored every nook and corner of London and was filled with wonder and fascination with all I saw! The London Underground seemed like a 'marvel' to me, for it was safe, fast, invariably on time and spotlessly clean in 1974! My friend gave me some pointers on how to navigate and find my way around the city and it was surprisingly easy for me to get around and explore various parts of the city about which I had read a lot as a student of literature. The cleanliness and organization of the city were particularly striking.

I then shifted to a hotel once my official visit started, and I had a British Council Guide assigned to me. He showed me around The British Museum, Natural History Museum, The Tower of London and other places of interest. My first visit outside London was to Dorset in "Hardy country". It was thrilling for me to see for myself places I had read described so vividly by Hardy in his novels like Jude, the Obscure, Tess, Under the Greenwood Tree and many others. So many places and situations described in the novels came streaming back to me! Finally, as I had long wished, I was able to visit Cambridge and Oxford universities, two hallowed places of learning. It appeared to me as if every student and teacher I came across seemed deeply absorbed in their work, and there was almost a perfect silence in each building. It was not the silence that resulted from fear or enforcement but the silence that represented scholarship, respect for others and traditions, and the pursuit of excellence.

I secretly wondered about how wonderful it would be if our seats of learning in India could also be like that. I got an opportunity to talk to students and faculty members, and I found them focused and motivated; in all of them, I detected a sense that they wanted their work and study to mean something! The campuses were invariably quiet but not silent! Those walking along the paths and passages never talked loudly. Just as one gets the sense of what is to come in the hushed and respectful tones in a meditation hall right before the instructor calls everyone to attention and the meditation practice begins, the air in these institutions had that same quality, one that was conducive to both study and reflection.

After the pilgrimage to Oxford and Cambridge, I travelled by train to Stafford for four days, and I found Staffordshire schools to be excellent. In fact, I sat in on a few classes and also had some brief interactions with the students there. As it transpired, many of them had not heard or read much about India besides some surface-level stereotypes, as was often the case, especially in that day and age!

I went out of the way and spoke to them about India's quickening pace of economic progress — both industrial and agricultural — and the strides India had already made in education at all levels. They were somewhat surprised, and dare I say, some of them were even impressed with what they heard from me about this vast, exotic, distant country! That part of England is famous for pottery, and I was shown around some pottery units. Now, with that being the Arnold Bennett area, I was once again quite interested in travelling around, as he was one of the pre-eminent writers we had studied while in university back home!

Next up was an extended stay in Yorkshire, where I attended a multinational, residential three-week program organized by the British Council on the Teaching of English as a Foreign Language at the University of Leeds. The attendees were all experienced teachers from countries where English was not the native or first language. The faculties were drawn from the University of Leeds and other universities, including the well-known London University Institute of Education. The faculty members were all exemplary with no exception, and their lectures were inspiring and Tutorials useful.

The concept of a "Language laboratory" was a novel concept at that time, and I found it most insightful and interesting! A highlight for me was the time we spent under the guidance of Prof. Brian Page, a pioneer in the field. We also had the opportunity to work with Prof. Peter McCarthy, a student of Daniel Jones, the "demi-God" of pronunciation, whose Pronouncing Dictionary is an authoritative compilation to this day! I made excellent use of this opportunity to clarify and seek counsel on a few issues concerning language teaching, and I benefited a great deal.

The three weeks in Leeds went by in a flash. There was so much to learn, and the nature of the program provided ample space for one to clarify one's ideas about a variety of subjects by interacting in an intimate setting with world-renowned scholars, generous with their time. This also helped me update and upskill my teaching methodologies and approaches. Speaking of updating one's skills, I must make particular mention of the concept of In-Service Training (INSET) for teachers that I learnt about while in the UK. INSET was considered an important element when a teacher was a candidate to be promoted to a higher post. Basically, one had to clock a minimum number of INSET hours before even being considered for a higher post. I strongly feel that this is a critical missing link in Indian education! Teachers need to constantly learn and update their skills. Otherwise, they run the risk of remaining stuck in the past without learning about new research on learning/teaching, novel methods of instruction and the evolving needs of children in a fast-moving society.

As Stephen Covey famously says, "Sharpen your saw!" Every trade and vocation calls for practitioners to constantly keep up with changes, make improvements and employ more optimal tools to further the discourse just a little more than the year before. Champion sportsmen/women do not keep winning if they do not evolve, just as surgeons cannot rely on training received in medical school alone! And so it is dangerous for the system if the teacher is not learning and eventually, he/she vegetates. The ultimate sufferers are the students, who also are our future citizens and leaders of the country and world at large! And so, upskilling of teachers is arguably even more critical than other professions! Especially in India, we collectively need to take this up on a massive scale, considering our vast numbers.

There were several "take home points" as they were from the schools I visited on this trip. At the end of my official programme, I paid a brief visit to Paris travelling overnight by train to the port city of Dover and then ship to cross the English Channel to the French port of Calais. There was a lot to see in Paris – world-renowned museums, including the Mona Lisa at the Louvre Museum, exquisite art centres, the beautiful Seine River, including the "Paris by night" cruise, the iconic Eiffel Tower and the majestic Arc de Triomphe on the Champs Elysees which commemorates those who had died during the French Revolution among many other sights. I felt really enriched by the visit, and I was mildly amused to see that the French were more helpful and friendly if I spoke Hindi or Telugu when I asked for directions, as opposed to English! Food, of course, was challenging for a vegetarian like me in France in the 1970s, but all in all, it was a whirlwind visit filled with memorable sights and experiences.

I have returned to the UK and Europe many times over since that visit. On a subsequent visit in 1982, I, along with four other Indian principals (on behalf of the Indian Public Schools Conference), visited Cambridge University for discussions with the Cambridge Overseas Board, the highly acclaimed Public Schools of Eton and Winchester, as well as the Manchester Grammar School and United World College of the Atlantic. I would marvel at how meticulously my hosts planned the school schedule. We sat in on classes and were even invited to teach a few classes! It was an interesting experience for me to teach students who were somewhat unfamiliar with me and the place I came from but yet freely asked questions and were curious to learn more! After all, it was only by encouraging students to ask questions that we made our teaching more meaningful. That way, it was a two-way traffic, so to speak, where we got to learn about practices in each other's country. We had useful meetings at Cambridge, where we managed to convince the officials that the Indian "10+2" curriculum was indeed equivalent to the "A levels" of the UK and that our school leavers would be eligible to join universities in the UK where their learning levels were at-par with any British student. This was a great takeaway that we were proud of!

On this visit in 1982, I also got to spend a few days at the Bharatiya Vidya Bhavan (Institute of Indian Culture) in London. As it turned out, the President of the Bhavan, Mr. C. Subramanyam, who had just retired from public office as Union Minister for Food and Agriculture, where he was largely responsible for ushering the Green Revolution, which made India self-sufficient, also happened to be visiting the Bhavan in London when I was there. Mr. S. Ramakrishnan, Director General of the Bhavan, was also present there. It was an opportunity of a lifetime for me to learn from and interact with these two stalwarts. Subramanyamji shared his experiences of working with Nehru and Indira Gandhi as I listened, wide-eyed and full of awe! Ramakrishnanji, on the other hand, had worked with Sardar Patel and K.M. Munshi before the Bhavan was founded. Both of them took me under their wing and were personally kind to me even as they imparted wisdom and information about a plethora of topics ranging from education policy and the art of institution building to the food policy of a nation and the impact it had on millions!

I also had the opportunity to visit Belgium, Switzerland, Germany, and the Netherlands on that trip, experienced the sights and sounds they had to offer, and had several interesting conversations with people from varied walks of life! When I eventually returned home after this three-month visit of learning and new experiences, I had made many friends for life and memories that last to this day! There was much I learnt as a young Head could learn from the methods and practices of my peers in the UK and Europe. From the value of ensuring continuous enrichment of my fellow teachers to fostering the remarkable spirit of curiosity of students, I witnessed everywhere how meticulous planning characterized every aspect of school administration and how traditions were preserved alongside the imperative to embrace new learnings and innovations! It was a fascinating time in my life as an idealistic and young principal, and I brought a lot of those learnings home with me to implement in the Indian context!

|CHAPTER 12|

Many Passages between India and the UK!

In Sept. 1984, the British Council, Bombay, requested me to take care of a Visitor from England, Mr. Michael Henley, County Education Officer, Northamptonshire, who would be spending a day in Baroda; I picked him up from the hotel and showed him around Baroda. We visited the Faculty of Education and the English department, where he interacted with professors, some of whom had studied in British universities such as Manchester, Leeds and London. He greatly enjoyed the exchanges.

We visited the Laxmi Vilas Palace, a fixture for any visitor to Baroda with any interest in history, culture or architecture and like everyone else seeing it for the first time, it was nothing short of magnificent in his eyes! Over the course of lunch, which included delicacies from Gujarat and Andhra Pradesh, where we hailed from, he got to meet Sheela, my wife, who was a well-known writer in Telugu, a major Indian language. He marvelled at the ease and fluency with which Sheela could articulate complex nuances from Telugu literature into English. Michael was always open to learning from people he had just met about their perspectives and life experiences they brought with them besides sharing his own, and these were precisely the kind of interactions he was looking for and longing to further!

That evening, after a hectic day spent visiting classrooms and talking to teachers and students, we were having tea on the lawn of the principal's bungalow, which was our home in those days. It was then that Mr. Henley asked, seemingly out of the blue, if we both would be open to the idea of visiting Northamptonshire for a few weeks the following summer. The idea would be to visit schools and talk to teachers and students as part of Northamptonshire's multicultural education. He assured us that the County Education Department of Northamptonshire would make all arrangements for our stay, boards, visits to schools, and other places of interest and that he would personally ensure that we felt at home and welcome. That night, over dinner, he began fleshing out what a trip for Sheela and I would look like, what he was hoping Northamptonshire School could benefit from, what we would find interesting and how logistics could be worked out. The pace at which it all began coming together took us by surprise!

As we were taking leave the next day, we presented him a small memento of something quintessentially Indian - a model of the Taj Mahal, of course! He was overjoyed! We promised to be in touch, work out the details and meet in England the following September! There was a lot to learn from how he visited new places and made connections instantly and instinctively, as well as observing keenly with a view to learning. As a senior education officer, he also made quick decisions to forge professional contacts with another country for which he clearly had great respect.

Soon after, Sheela and I started our plans to go to the UK in September of 1985. We prepared the material on Multicultural Education for what was to be a month-long visit. We left for London in the first week of September 1985 and were received at Heathrow by the Inspector of the County Education Office, Northamptonshire, Rashida Spencer. Rashida would go on to become a close personal friend over the decades to come! She told us that Michael had requested her to take charge of all arrangements and programmes concerning our trip. Rashida, whose family had migrated to the UK from East Africa, had a good idea of India, thanks in part to her Indian heritage and that made Sheela feel at home instantly!

We stayed in the town of Wellingborough, Northamptonshire, where Sheela was attached to a Junior School based there, whereas a teacher would drive me down each morning to the town of Northampton, which was ten miles away, where I would go on to work in a few different schools over the course of our visit. We would invariably have lunch with the students, teachers and Headteacher of the school, and these were a wonderful way for us to have conversations, learn from each other and understand the nuances, challenges and intricacies of school education in the UK. It is amazing how much one learns from informal discussions and organic interactions!

Sheela and I would organise INSET (In Service Education and Training) for groups of teachers from various schools on Saturday mornings. We would talk about various aspects of education with particular reference to India. We soon learnt that the quality of our talk could easily be gauged by how much follow-up discussion we would end up having! If nobody had a question or the follow-up discussion was not lively and engaging, we would have to do a better job next time!

What we found particularly moving and humbling was how the Indian community in Wellingborough opened up their hearts and homes to us. Every single evening during our stay there, a different family invited us for dinner, where over delicious food, we would talk about India, the UK, and the unique facets of living in a multicultural Britain where the parents and grandparents were often born in India or East Africa while the children were born in the UK!

Time passed quickly and happily, and Sheela and I learnt a lot about school education in Northamptonshire, the curriculum, school organisation, INSET, and other Saturday morning activities for teachers. We had a few review meetings with Michael Henley both on our own and with his senior officials present. Both he and we were happy about the way our programme was going. Michael and his wife, Wendy, invited Sheela and me to their home for a few meals, which were wonderful and intimate. Little did we imagine how the sequence of events would unfold and bring us to Northamptonshire as just a few months ago; we knew very little about him or him about us! Such is the glorious unpredictability of life and the wondrous journeys it enables us to undertake!

Soon, it was time to bid farewell to our wonderful hosts in Wellingborough and the teachers and students who had opened their hearts and minds to us. We made so many new friends and learnt much about the differences and similarities in our education systems, our challenges, and our shared ideas of what we hold important and want our children to learn!

A few days before our departure, Sheela and I invited a team of educationists from Northamptonshire to visit us in India for a month. And sure enough, Michael Henley immediately confirmed that several teachers, Headteachers and other educationists had expressed to him that they would be very interested in visiting India! And, based on the positive feedback from us, our host schools, and the community, Michael also suggested we visit the UK a second time! We had not yet finished the first visit when we were already talking about coming back! Of course, before that, there was the small matter of hosting a large British party and giving them a feel for Indian education, culture and hospitality, just as we had experienced the same during our delightful couple of months in the summer of 1985 in the UK, which will remain etched in our memories forever.

Accordingly, the next year, a group of educationists from Northamptonshire visited India and came to Baroda for a week. Before coming to us, they visited Delhi, Agra, Jaipur and some national parks and sanctuaries for two weeks. Parents and well-wishers of the school leaned in and supported this visit wholeheartedly. We put our British friends up in various guest houses, which were the most comfortable. I deputed some of my senior colleagues to take great care of them. As is often the case, various friendships took shape during these interactions — some expected and others less so — and that was one of the most gratifying parts of building these cross-national collaborations and the goodwill and positive energy they unleashed!

We arranged visits for them to places of interest in and around Baroda. They visited the M.S. University, where we set up a meeting with the Vice-Chancellor. They also spent a lot of time in the school interacting with our teachers and even taught a few classes and sat in on others. While it was a new experience for our students and staff, our guests were left impressed with the high standards our school had set in academics as well as visual and performing arts and sports. They even joined the students and played cricket, football, tennis, hockey and other games! Gentle banter about our national cricket teams and who was better would often ensue, and it was all great fun!

Our British friends learnt some Indian songs and dances. After a programme of music and dance by the students, we would sit down and eat dinner together. We took them to the well-known AMUL Dairy in Anand, where, after a tour of the facility, we had a meeting with Dr. V. Kurien, the Chairman, a visionary who was considered the father of the "White Revolution", as some called it. Our visitors were enthralled by Dr. Kurien's vision, depth of knowledge, involvement and organisational ability. It gave them a unique vantage point from which to study and get a feel for Indian industry and society.

Soon, their week with us was over, and they left for Bombay and went back home. They all felt the visit to India was a rich learning experience. Our students, staff, and parents were enthused and motivated, too, as they saw through the eyes of our British visitors that we had indeed built a high-quality, diverse, well-rounded institution that could hold its own in the world!

Soon enough, we paid a return visit to the UK in the summer of 1988, and this time, we spent two or three days in a given school and stayed with the Headteacher. Sheela was attending junior schools, and I was in senior sections, spending most of my time with the Headteacher. We would interact a great deal on aspects of school administration, the issues he had to face, and dealing with challenging students and teachers. We found it not only interesting but also realised that the issues were not vastly dissimilar to those we, as administrators or teachers, faced back in India. In addition, Sheela taught groups of children a few dances and songs. The power of music and dance as mediums to build bridges and understand the lives and cultures of others never ceases to amaze me! Our hosts showed us around Oxford and Cambridge and took us to a Shakespeare play at Stratford-on-Avon. Sheela and I gave a few talks on India and the Indian culture, and the students and teachers interacted with us freely, and it was a mutual learning experience. Our son, who tagged along on this second UK visit, got to experience a bit of English school and family life! Once again, a delightful and vibrant few weeks in Northamptonshire strengthened our bonds with old friends and enabled us to forge new friendships, some that continue to this day, decades later!

We returned to Baroda and soon after began preparations for the return visit of a second group of English educationists who would spend 10 days in Baroda. We once again activated our network of supporters, parents and well-wishers and made similar arrangements for their stay in comfortable guest houses. They spent even more time in the school than the first group had and interacted freely with our teachers and students. We showed them around Baroda and also gave them a tour of Gujarat. We organised a meeting for them with no less than the Chief Minister of the State! Our British visitors were once again welcomed by our students, staff and parents with open arms. The visitors were delighted to visit an Indian home, interact with the hosts, and have a meal with them, which was typically a Gujarati meal with distinct flavours. Visiting couples and host families invariably exchanged gifts, and while these were often inexpensive, they were thoughtfully chosen by both sides and provided a segue into deeper conversations and connections!

Several lasting friendships were formed, and over time, these relationships grew and, in some cases, there were follow-up visits in either direction! This aspect of these UK-India exchanges gave me immense pleasure especially since the school had brought people together towards something authentic and organic that stood the test of time!

Each time our visitors bid farewell from India, or we took leave from our hosts in the UK, it reminded me about the importance of nurturing such exchanges of people and ideas and the shared understanding it builds on both sides! Indeed, this is how we grow as people, institutions and nations!

|CHAPTER 13|

Exchanges and Beyond!

Little did I know that the Northamptonshire exchanges in the mid to late 80s were only the beginning of what was to be a series of exchanges in the months and years to follow! During our stay in Northamptonshire, Sheela and I grew particularly fond of the Northampton School for Boys (NSB), a highly rated school, and we got to know its Headmaster, Bruce Liddington, rather well. He was a young, dynamic and strategic thinker, and Bruce immediately suggested that we set up a student-to-student exchange between our two schools.

We welcomed the first group of five boys and a teacher from NSB. We arranged for them to stay with boys whose parents took care of the visitors, treating them just like their children. The teacher escort stayed in the school guest house and kept in close touch with the boys. The visitors attended classes, and the teacher taught a few lessons and sat in on a few classes, observing our approaches to teaching, which indeed were not very different from their country. There were plenty of discussions between them, which I felt were mutually beneficial, and many prejudices disappeared, and clarity was established. We arranged for our visiting party to travel to places of interest like Delhi, Agra, Jaipur and the tiger reserve in Ranthambore. They also took part in the sport of their choice and cultural activities like music, dance and art. We arranged a cultural evening on their last day when our students and visiting students together presented a wonderful programme followed by dinner at the principal's bungalow.

After the resounding success of NSB visiting India, our student group and a teacher paid a return visit to Northampton the following year and had a similar programme. Thus, the exchange continued for a few years. Many students, teachers and parents participated and made the exchanges richer and more meaningful with each passing visit! In fact, the exchange even continued after I left Bhavan's Baroda and moved to Daly College in Indore. But, sadly, as it happens with many initiatives like these exchanges, when I retired and Bruce left the school for another assignment, the exchange came to a halt. It was a reminder that traditions, just like relationships, take great effort and care so they thrive and stand the test of time!

Thanks to many of the relationships Sheela and I were fortunate to have built over the years with these visits back and forth, I was introduced to and eventually invited to attend the Secondary Heads Association (SHA) Conference, where I spoke on various aspects of school education in India. Members attending the SHA conference were curious and sensitive about incorporating perspectives from a broad spectrum of contributors. They were appreciative of my talks and eventually made me an Honorary Fellow of SHA. Staying true to the tradition of setting up and nurturing exchanges, I promptly invited some of the British Heads to the annual conclave of the Indian Public Schools Conference. Three British friends went on to attend the conclave and then dropped in to visit my school. We were now experts at this drill, and we showed them around places of interest, facilitated discussions with our staff and engaged in long conversations on a range of topics, none more pertinent than the challenges of school education and the art and craft of building the leaders and citizens of tomorrow! In case there was any doubt, I could confirm that Sheela and I loved every aspect of setting up, planning and executing each of these rich and multi-layered exchanges!

Following the SHA conference and the reciprocal visits by British friends to India, I was organically introduced to the newly formed International Confederation of Principals (ICP), and before I knew it, I was representing India and had been invited to speak at the first Conference held at Geneva, Switzerland in 1993 where I spoke on the topic of "Education for Human Happiness" which was well received. The second conference was held in Sydney, Australia, where I spoke on "The Emerging Role of the Principal in the New Century". That conference was held in 1995 just as we were getting ready to meet the challenges of the new century. The third ICP session was held in Boston, Massachusetts, in 1997, where I spoke on "The Importance of Value Education". Naturally, my talk gave an Indian perspective on the topic, and there was a lively discussion after the talk.

My participation in these ICP sessions enabled me to meet several people worldwide, and I was invited to a few countries to address their principals. For instance, I was invited to Helsinki to speak at the Finnish Principals' National Convention. Though it was very cold in Scandinavia in the month of November, the President of the Association was a wonderful host who took special care of my dietary needs. The Education Minister of Finland was in the audience during my presentation on "Importance of Value Education in Schools". Because of the weather, I could get only a glimpse of the beautiful city of Helsinki, which I had heard and read so much about. To my surprise, I found that the Finnish people spoke fluent and flawless English! Another fact that struck me about Finland was the high level of satisfaction that the Fins had with how their government worked for the benefit of all its people and also particularly striking was how young people who held positions of responsibility across the board were. This suggested to me a bright future for the country.

Then, there was another example of what was merely a chance encounter on the sidelines of the Boston ICP conference that led to a long and fruitful association. A senior Principal from Australia named Duncan Stalker and I met, got into a conversation on a range of topics, including cricket, of course, and soon after, he evinced a keen interest in his school and a possible visit to Daly College, Indore in a first of its kind "cricket exchange" especially since both Australia and India were passionate about cricket. I readily agreed, knowing that my school, Daly College, took pride in maintaining high standards of cricket and had a glorious history, including several old boys who played for India after their schooling with us. We worked out the modalities, and I invited the Australian group to visit us first, and we would pay a return visit the following year.

Duncan himself arrived with their cricket team, and I went all the way to Delhi and received the party. After a brief visit to Delhi, our visiting party arrived at Indore to a grand welcome. The visiting team from Brauer College, Victoria and my school team played an enthralling game of cricket that the visitors won. We arranged a rolling trophy named the "Laxman Singh Trophy", and the winning team got to keep it till the next fixture. Laxman Singh, an old Dalian, was a great batsman of his time, and fittingly, we invited him to present the Trophy. We even named the new ground where the game was played "The Laxman Singh Oval" in his honour.

After a week of sightseeing, our visitors went back home, but not before they had made wonderful friends on and off the field. They created and left us with memories that would last a long time. The following year, we visited Australia and played at Brauer College. And just like Duncan had done, Sheela and I escorted the team to Australia. This time, to our delight, our team emerged victorious! Our hosts were quite gracious, and we visited the beautiful city of Melbourne and the iconic Sydney Harbour and Opera House, among other sights. We returned home with the Laxman Singh Trophy to a tumultuous welcome. The cricket exchange continued for a few years and eventually stopped after Duncan retired in Victoria, and I retired from Daly College. However, the personal ties between the families continued for many years. Something I learnt about the Australians stayed with me years later — that they took even friendly fixtures most seriously and gave it their all. Their passion for competing and their appetite for winning struck me as an admirable quality. However, off the field, they were warm, hospitable and charming.

Brauer College, Australia Hosts the Daly College (Indore) Cricket Team, Circa 2000

Finally, the last foreign collaboration I need to mention is the one that was, in some ways, the most unlikely! My son, Srinadh, was studying his graduation in Engineering at the De Montfort University, Leicester, and I visited him whenever I visited England on work. Like all parents, I, too, was interested in learning more about his department and University, so I would drop in and try the faculty if they had time. During these encounters, the Dean of Engineering, Graham Chapman and I became great friends, and not long after, I invited him to India to address the annual IPSC conclave. Graham readily agreed and soon after came to India. We took him to a few places of interest, and he developed great regard for India. It was during a long flight that we shared the idea of setting up a collaborative business school. On his return to the UK, he discussed the proposal with his vice-chancellor, who was quite supportive of the idea.

Graham then wrote and invited me to Leicester for further discussions. Before I knew it, I was visiting Leicester for a week, and Graham took me to the vice-chancellor, who seemed keen on starting a Business School in collaboration with The Daly College at Indore. I later had extensive discussions with a group of DMU faculty and administrators constituted by him for this ambitious and new project! We discussed a lot of details and finally arrived at some clarity and also came out with a time-bound plan of action. I returned to India and took the final clearance from my Board of Governors, who were also keen and supportive of the idea of starting a new institution in collaboration with DMU, UK.

Finally, I invited Graham to visit us with the Dean of Business from DMU to finally shape the proposal and fine-tune our decisions. Meanwhile, Graham was appointed as the director of the newly created International Office. That helped matters even more, and we worked out our final proposal. A student had to pass 12th Boards with a minimum 60% aggregate, study at the newly started Daly College Business School (DCBS) for two years and go to Leicester for the final year. After passing, the student would be awarded a B.A. (Honours) Business Administration by De Montfort University. The programme was a huge success, and many students got into good jobs after graduation, and some later studied MBA in the UK, USA or India. As a small personal aside, DMU decided to bestow upon me an Honorary Doctorate in Education, which was a testament to the wonderful collaboration we were able to start and nourish over the years!

Receiving Honorary Doctorate in Education at De Montfort University, Leicester UK, 2000

Subsequently, I have heard that efforts are being made to start an MBA degree at DCBS. The DCBS project has been a source of immense pride and joy, given how new the idea was at that time and how little things could have become major roadblocks. Thanks to an earnest and sincere friend and partner, Graham, we smoothed over every challenge and set in motion what was to become a dream project for us and so many who benefitted from this unique collaboration!

SECTION V:

Looking Back At It All and Passing It Forward

|CHAPTER 14|

Striking the Balance!

It is important for a school, or for that matter, any institution, as years pass, to usher in changes with changing times. However, it is also vital to keep in mind that the purpose and philosophy of the school are preserved. Striking this balance between preserving the ethos and fundamental fabric of a school even as we adapt, modernise and indeed begin anew where appropriate is one of the most important things a school Head has to help navigate. T.S. Eliot artfully calls it "Tradition and the Individual Talent." He says, "This historical sense, which is a sense of the timeless as well as the temporal together, is what makes a writer transitional. And it is at the same time what makes a writer most acutely conscious of his place in time, of his own contemporaneity."

The same is true of a school and, for that matter, any dynamic institution. What we are envisaging is not change for the sake of change but change with the changing world! One example is the intelligent use of technology in education. Can we make use of modern gadgets, ever-improving models of artificial intelligence, or vast amounts of data and its analytics without students becoming lost, overwhelmed, or merely props? This is one of the most important questions of the times we live in, and as leaders of schools, we have to grapple with and sort out. Let's not blindly ADOPT what the gadgets can do but ADAPT them to our needs and situations! Chat GPT doing the work of our children is not what we are after;

rather, we should equip our children to make enlightened choices about where AI can help them, where technology might help overcome obstacles or gaps in our understanding of difficult problems or indeed where they treat technology with respect and awe but also with a mild sense of scepticism and caution! As a result, our task is cut out to ensure our school leavers are well-equipped to deal with changing situations and yet not lose what is relevant in tradition!

Beyond technology, we all know that good infrastructure is critically important for a school. Indeed, it is a necessary ingredient of any school that takes pride in fostering excellence, both for students and teachers, not just for academic purposes but also for co-curricular activities and administrative functions. There is always a danger that school management gets lost in over-providing this and losing sight of what all this is in service of! While infrastructure is absolutely necessary, we should also remember that it is not the be-all and end-all of a school. While "hardware" is necessary, it is vital to have top-class "human software" to sustain a school.

Teachers must be qualified and have a flair for teaching and, above all, must enjoy the company of children and wish to see them learn and succeed! One of the key functions of a Head is to recruit the best talent in terms of the right type of teachers and then train them in various ways. And training is not a one-time thing by any means. There must be regular and ongoing "in service" programmes that update the knowledge base and awareness of teachers with the latest developments in subject matter content and the pedagogy and methodology of teaching each subject. Regular faculty meetings are essential, too, and are often overlooked or deprioritised in favour of the most critical burning subject of the day! So, not only do they need to happen on a regular basis, but the principal himself/herself should attend to them by turns. The heads of departments, too, should be required to hold regular meetings where matters concerning a specific subject or set of subjects and any broader learning or feedback are discussed and incorporated. When possible, specialists from the local university or outside experts should be invited to address these meetings. Finally, good educationists of repute must be invited to interact with teachers at the monthly staff meetings. As mentioned in the Northamptonshire writings, Sheela and I attended these meetings at schools in England and greatly enjoyed the follow-up interactions and Q&A sessions. These are called INSET (in Service Training) programmes. In the UK, they have gone a step further and made it essential for a teacher to have attended a certain number of these programmes to be even eligible for promotion in their cadre! I would urge that similar programmes be organised in India as part of the system. As a management expert says, "Sharpen the saw!" While such learning programmes are essential for all professions, it is even more vital in ours as we are entrusted with the future treasure of the country!

The philosophy and ethos of the school must be clearly understood by all the teachers, and in addition to the Head being the only one telegraphing this, senior teachers also have a very important role in this. There needs to be zero confusion about the mission and guiding principles of the institution. It is vitally important to keep re-emphasising this because if the philosophy is not clear to a section of teachers, they will continue doing their work blindly, which will be unfortunate!

Here again, the Head must carefully ensure that everyone works with the philosophy in mind at all times.

Inculcating the right type of relationship between students and teachers is again of utmost importance. If there is a fundamental level of trust and transparency in this relationship, many problems can be avoided, and the educational process will go on smoothly. The soul of the institution lies in these relationships – not just between teachers and students but also between the Head and the teachers, the students and the parents, and the community in general. The Head must forge this in all contacts, both internal and external, and only then will the school and the Head be successful.

Although there is a need for a well-laid-out structure in a school for it to function properly, this does not need to be followed rigidly at all costs. Every member of staff, at any level of seniority or rank, should be fully empowered and be able to reach the Head or Deputy Head at any time to talk over official matters or even, in some cases, personal problems as we are dealing with human beings with real lives and real problems! While access to this should exist, it should not be used indiscriminately, and when a staff member does meet anyone, the conversation should be cordial, serious, earnest and responsible. For that matter, this should happen as a matter of course — among the staff, the students and even parents. Communication of the right type and, indeed, a two-way conversation is the lifeblood of a good school.

It is also important that the school has excellent public relations within the community where it operates. Strong public relations do not mean obliging the community for every favour they ask or setting boundaries to avoid them over-stepping and trying to interfere with the school's functioning! Once again, it is a delicate balance. The community must be made to feel that the school is theirs and that they need to support it in a positive manner with no expectation of anything in return! For instance, the community has to be involved in a healthy way if the school undertakes any fundraising programmes. Similarly, the school should maintain cordial relationships with local bureaucracy and political leaders. The Head has to do this with great care and maturity!

For example, at Bhavan's Baroda, we organised a number of benefit programmes by eminent musicians held on the school campus to raise funds for much-needed projects. We could manage this with the good offices of a few well-wishers of the school and friends. Pandit Ravi Shankar, in fact, gave two performances within a span of four years. Others who helped the school are Padma Subramaniam, the famous dancer, and Pandit Hari Prasad Chaurasia, the virtuoso flute player. The staff worked around the clock in some cases during these events, and this brought them closer and increased their pride in the school. These activities not only brought the staff and parents closer but also played a key role in cementing the strong relationship the school enjoyed within the community as well. This was an example of how Bhavan's Baroda had embraced this small change — just a few years before, it would have been unthinkable that a classical music concert of all things would be held on the school premises and it would end up enthralling audiences, building a strong sense of shared responsibility and creating goodwill for the school.

In this chapter, we have explored the balance between tradition and change a little. The other balance I had alluded to was having a structure and rules and knowing when to ease off slightly in invoking them blindly! We had what our teachers called a "problem student" at Indore. The teachers had reached the end of their patience with this student and wanted me to expel the boy from the school. This was four months before the Board exam. With an open mind, I listened to the teachers, and they described the various problems they had with him in detail. Finally, I called the boy to come and see me at home in the evening. To my surprise, we ended up having a good chat, and then he dropped a mini bombshell that left me a little stunned! He told me that he was facing criticism from a few teachers for problems which he actually did not have anything to do with! He also said that he had great faith in my fairness, and if my inquiries into the matter did not corroborate his version of the story, he said he was ready to face the consequences. He then left, and I was not quite sure why, but there had been a breakdown of communication between this child and his teachers, or at least some of them, for I heard different versions of the story from the teachers and the boy.

I thought over the issue during my evening walk. I told myself that it was quite plausible that both the teachers and the boy could be right at the same time, and instead of ascertaining who was more correct, the right thing to do here would be to defuse and de-escalate the situation as opposed to treat it like a court case! I telephoned his father, who promised to see me at school the next day. The parents met me and my Deputy the next day. He was profusely apologetic for his son having caused this misunderstanding and earnestly requested us to save his career. We assured him that, on the contrary, our chief concern was building the careers of students and helping them grow into good young men and women, bringing credit to their school and family. The parent felt heard and saw that besides understanding the frustration of our teachers on the matter, we also recognised his humanity and that of his son. He was moved to tears, stood up and told me with folded hands that he had never come across an educationist with such a positive approach before.

We called the boy next, who was visibly nervous. I went over the list of grievances our teachers had with the boy but also acknowledged that he had expressed his contrition even though he felt he had been misunderstood. I then asked my Deputy if he could take charge of the boy and advise/guide him in the days/weeks ahead. The boy's face brightened as he saw a ray of hope. The father then said he would take him home for a day, and he and his wife would counsel him in a proper manner and bring him back to school. They returned after a day, and I told the parent and the boy that I would give him a last chance, and the Deputy Head had graciously agreed to vouch for him and look after him. The boy's joy knew no bounds, and the father was moved to tears.

Thereafter, there was a marked change in the boy, and he is now doing very well in life. We all learned from this experience. While it is important to be fair and follow all rules, it is also my conviction and philosophy that we have to put people first. These rules have to ultimately help produce good human beings, and we have to allow room for humans to learn and grow sometimes!

|CHAPTER 15|

So, What Makes A Good Leader?

I have often been asked this question when it comes to school leadership: "What qualities does one need to have in order to be able to lead a school well?" It is a simple enough question, but there is no one single answer to it! It is said that there are certain "must haves" for a school principal. First and foremost, anyone who is a teacher or principal must have a genuine love for children. This is a non-negotiable prerequisite one should look for when hiring someone for the job of a teacher or principal. Knowledge and interest in child psychology are also necessary. In some situations, when the Head has to decide an issue and if there is room for a doubt, the benefit of the doubt must go to the child. That implies that the teacher and the Head have a healthy dose of underlying optimism about the future, which is essential for us to continue our work efficiently and cheerfully.

A good principal is guided at all times by a vision of the school, one that he/she will always carry out by involving all the stakeholders and creating a culture of sharing and teamwork every step of the way. Whatever is done at the school must be in tune with this shared vision. What is implicit here is that the vision is something that all stakeholders believe in, or else it becomes a top-down imposition of something that does not have broad support. So, creating an environment where everyone contributes to coming up with this shared vision and then plays their part in living up to it is essential. Once the staff of the school are bought into it, they will then go on to help students develop clarity and pride in the purpose of the school. How can one tell that a school has a vision that is widely shared and understood? I have sometimes been told by students in a school – "This is NOT done in our school!" or "This has to be done since it is an important part of the culture of our school." It was abundantly clear that in both instances, the students who said these had internalised the vision of their school and lived it day to day! It was no longer an abstract concept for them. That is how we know if the vision of a school has been shared and understood.

Another trait that I believe every good principal I have ever known has is being a lifelong learner! A school is a place of learning, and all concerned, including teachers and the Head, should be learning all the time. In fact, teaching in the real sense is learning. A teacher who is not learning while teaching is merely doling out "knowledge" and sooner or later is bound to be rejected or resisted by those who are at the receiving end of it. Learning implies teachers having a lively interaction with their students, and the teacher always looks at a topic afresh and imparts it in a lively manner as if it is the first time he/she is teaching it! That enthusiasm, love of the teaching/learning process and self-confidence are what rub off on students. That type of teacher is learning, and we want such lifelong learning Heads and teachers! A learning school of this kind is a happy place to be where everyone feels secure, vulnerable and respected.

Being open to revising one's decision is yet another hallmark of a good leader! We all have to make decisions sometimes based on incomplete information, and we are not always going to get it right. One hopes that good leaders get more decisions right than not, but what is also important is that upon realising that a particular choice they made was not the best decision, a Head must be open to changing it and acknowledging it as such to his colleagues. Indeed, I would argue that would enhance their respect. A good Head is also happy to receive constructive feedback from his/her colleagues, parents and even students! It is critical for Heads to cultivate what Psychologist Carol Dweck calls "the growth mindset."

A slight digression from the question of who makes a good principal to the term itself! It is interesting to see how our comprehension of what all being a principal entails has evolved over time. First, the job was viewed to be more of a "manager", but in time, it was felt that this definition implied a certain level of "top-down" thinking. It was then felt that he/she could be an "administrator", but then the title conveyed a certain level of detachment and officialdom that was not quite in keeping with the context of school education and preparing the citizens of tomorrow. In the course of time, it was felt that the principal should be a sort of "facilitator" who makes things easy for functioning, but that felt a little limiting in scope. Then, the principal was viewed as a "leader" who has the flavour of taking others along in work. However desirable all these titles are, the term "Principal' has come to stay. Simply put, the principal is the principal learner in a learning organisation, which is a school! It is felt by some educationists that a good way to look at it is to consider the Head to be more of a "statesman" (or indeed "stateswoman"); a statesman is a mature person with a clear vision and enjoys the respect of everyone. We really need our principals to function like statesmen.

The other perspective that a good principal is mindful of is that a school is, in essence, a collaborative relationship among all individuals involved in the endeavour and it is the job of the principal to create a happy and conducive atmosphere based on trust and a spirit of shared responsibility. This feeling of oneness is essential for the success of the school. Constant interaction with everyone can help a great deal. So, a principal must be an excellent communicator. As Covey says, "Seek first to understand, then to be understood." When a person comes to say something to the Head, he/she must enable this person to say all he/she has on his/her mind and only then must the principal offer his/her response. Often, problems arise because the student or the teacher feels the Head is too busy talking and does not listen! Communication must be ongoing and a two-way street, as they say.

Thinking outside the box is also a sign of a great principal. For instance, I had no idea that something like organising group health insurance and Mediclaim would go a long way to create a happy atmosphere in the school! I also know of a school which gives loans to teachers at nominal interest for buying a vehicle (a car or a scooter, for instance), and as a result, almost every member of staff owns their own vehicle. This, in turn, has driven up morale and a sense of ownership! Providing students with opportunities for leadership training is another reliable way to build a larger circle of trust in the school. Leadership training may even be something as simple as senior students taking school visitors around during their free periods. This invariably increases their pride in their school and also fosters a sense of belonging. The school can even host a Model United Nations (MUN) session and invite other schools to join, where each participant or a small group represents a country. The participants develop self-confidence, and activities like this are necessary for personality growth.

There is an old saying — "If you haven't laughed for a whole day, you have wasted the day!" A teacher must have a sense of humour and, most of all must feel secure and comfortable laughing at themselves on occasion, too. There is an oversimplification that the essence of teaching is a sense of humour. But humour does play a part, and it is an important one. I once had a colleague who was a brilliant mathematics teacher but was also slightly absent-minded. He once walked into the class and announced: "Students, I want to tell you I am going to give you a surprise test tomorrow!" This made the students burst into laughter, and when he realised what he had said, he joined them in laughing! When he started teaching, every student paid full attention. I cite this as an example to emphasise the role played by humour in teaching.

Being tactful and diplomatic are vastly underrated qualities in my book! Ultimately, a principal is a leader of and among people and deals with people, so these two qualities are of vital importance. Interested and engaged parents? Yes! Overreaching and interfering parents? No, thank you! The principal should carefully avert this and one way to do that would be by involving chosen parents to help with activities where they work with the teachers and contribute their talents. In this way, the parents develop a sense of ownership and are more likely to see themselves as partners and allies of the school and the Head as opposed to a dynamic where they feel they need to opine on any and every aspect of the functioning of the institution. This parental involvement programme should be carefully constructed and monitored by the principal and a few senior teachers. Thus, gradually, what can be parental interference turns into healthy parental involvement! The principal will soon learn the art of dealing with various types of parents—ambitious, over-concerned, those who constantly compare their children with other children, those who always watch over their children, who we can call helicopter parents and those who are full of self-importance! In the end, we must realise that while parents are a vital part of the school, we must also ensure that they are satisfied but do not end up controlling the institution in any way. The school can also organise Reading Clubs for interested parents so that they respect the school and the staff. Once this relationship is established, the problems will be minimised and slowly eliminated. The key to any relationship is trust, and once this begins to grow, the school becomes a happy place.

Finally, the principal must be a person of unquestioned integrity. He/she should not accept gifts or solicit favours from anyone. I know of a principal who never entered the exam wing when his own child was taking the Board exam. He, thus, set an example to others and won their appreciation and respect. Such exemplary behaviour can inspire students, too, and will go a long way in instilling values in them. After all, values are transmitted to children by parents at home and teachers at school. Values cannot be taught through lectures. Sometimes, it is a happy revelation to me that we could lay the foundation for a strong value system for growing students. To stand for what is right is the basis of a strong value system. In their work, the principals influence and change many colleagues. Thus, the principal and the school become a sort of "change-maker" and "character builder".

A UNESCO Commission Report on "LEARNING: THE TREASURE WITHIN" was brought out in 1996. The Commission was headed by Jacques Delor and had some eminent thinkers from a few countries on it. Karan Singh from India was a member, and the main task of the Commission was to make recommendations on relevant education for the 21st century. The epoch-making report, among other aspects, stressed the following:

- Learning to know
- Learning to do
- Learning to learn together
- Learning to be

A good principal should have the above-mentioned encompassing aspects as the guiding principle for the educational endeavour. In Karan Singh's words, "Holistic education must acknowledge the multiple dimensions of human personality—physical, intellectual, aesthetic, emotional and spiritual—thus moving towards the perennial dream of an integrated living on a harmonious planet."

|CHAPTER 16|

What Makes a School Good?

What do we mean by a good school, and, in turn, what makes a school good? These are excellent questions that I have been asked from time to time and something that I have thought about, discussed and come up with each time I have visited these topics! So, these questions need to be unpacked and examined in a little detail.

First and foremost, for a school to even be eligible for the "good" category, the school should have teachers who love children! Then, the school has to be a learning institution in the true sense of the word where everyone associated with it is learning constantly — the students, the teachers, and the Head. It also means an atmosphere of openness, sharing, inclusivity and receptivity to suggestions and new ideas. A spirit of excellence and high standards of learning not only exists but pervades the place!

A good school endeavours to provide the students with a wholesome education — a high standard of academics, adequate attention given to cultural pursuits, a range of sports and community service. It is vital for the growing children to feel they are loved and respected and that their work is valued. A good school ensures that traditions, procedures, and routines are clearly articulated and that all involved proudly follow them. A good school values rules and norms but is not afraid to change them where and if needed after a robust discussion. A good school does not trumpet for what it is but rather derives its status and currency from what it means to the people who make it what it is!

Parents play a huge part in determining how good a school is. They naturally have a strong interest in the school and want to see it succeed, but at times, they can be too invested in the school, which can lead to them having an appetite to tell the Head what to do, how to do it and when! I arrived at my own way of dealing with parents — I would discuss the school with them up to a point, but there are some areas that are best not discussed with them. There was a proverbial "Lakshman Rekha" that we all understood and followed. So, we involved the parents in sharing their skills for a fixed time during school time. Some who were sportsmen would work with the school coaches and enrich the standard of the game.

In terms of the "hardware" aspect, a good infrastructure and facilities are necessary, as we have discussed already. It is also critical to ensure that they provide values of space and a connection to the Earth. So, again, a great deal of planning and discussions would need to go into building infrastructure, maintaining it, and modernising it periodically. We often see that with the passage of time, buildings and facilities break down and cut a sorry figure compared to when they were first put up. Nothing is more depressing for a child than seeing the school campus they study in is not tended to. Just like every beautiful garden needs a gardener constantly caring for it and working hard to maintain it, school campuses and infrastructure, too, need careful and enlightened stewardship and utmost care.

Every good school I have seen is authentic and does not feel the need to be good in someone else's estimation but in its own. And no matter how many laurels or accolades come its way, it needs to remain grounded, eager to learn, willing to course correct and keep going! We should always be proud of what we are doing, but we should always be open to learning, unlearning and relearning for growth. It is also imperative for a school to achieve excellent results in the right way and using the right means! This is a vital principle that has to be inculcated in all students and teachers. This is sometimes overlooked, especially as metrics do not capture or reflect the values that inform the charter and mission of the school!

Someone wisely pointed out that school stands for collective striving. All should understand that a vital factor in any institution is that all members stand together. I was very impressed to read the motto of the school: "Our school is four walls with tomorrow inside – where children think, dream, believe and achieve!" Thus, the school is a highly vital institution in society, which contains the future of not just the community or the nation but of the entire world. This devolves a tremendous responsibility on the Head and the teachers to mould their wards on the right lines so that they become world citizens.

Again, good schools take great care to groom and mould integrated individuals who are not just academically excelling students! Students take part in a sport of their choice as well as opportunities abound for participation and learning music, dance, and literary activities like debates, discussions and quiz programmes. The school library is usually well-stocked with a variety of books, and students are encouraged to read widely. Book clubs are organised, and slowly, this may lead to creative activities like poetry writing and writing short stories. The principal personally should attend these meetings to encourage those with creative propensities. The goal is to provide the students with an atmosphere where they can grow into fine, balanced individuals with empathy and concern for others.

A continuous dialogue between the staff and the students about various aspects of life and how they should face their future with intelligence and courage is another hallmark of a good school. We know we have done our part when we feel confident that our students would stand for values in any situation they encounter. That is a true character, and we should engage in co-building it with the children we are responsible for while they are at school for their future such that our students are recognised by their integrity, compassion, and invariably standing for what is right! Each student is provided with a challenge which he/she faces with confidence, a challenge which is not frustratingly difficult but one which she/he can cope with and learn. It has to be understood that excellence is a journey, not a destination. Past successes have to be put behind us, and new struggles have to be waged, and no setback is a permanent failure that cannot be recovered from!

Whether I liked it or not, I came to realise that a school is often synonymous with the Head, and so a principal has to tread carefully and lightly with humility and confidence. When one says it is a good school, we often factor in the fact that someone competent or trustworthy is leading the school as the principal. At the same time, I also understood that we, the teachers, have to continue to be co-learners with our colleagues and guide and train our colleagues as learning individuals, and in turn, all of us together strive to ensure that we have learning parents. This ambience of learning makes a 'good' school — a learning school.

One thing that my colleagues and I benefited from immensely was our discussion meetings — they provided ample space for group learning! Somehow, over the years, these meetings were called "study circles" by the teachers, and everyone participated in them with enthusiasm and keenness to learn. Once, one of the teachers brought a book by Krishnamurti and read a few lines from it to start off the discussion. I quote: "In our relationship with children and young people, we are not dealing with mechanical devices that can be quickly repaired, but with living beings who are impressionable, volatile, sensitive, afraid, affectionate; and to deal with them, we must have great understanding, the strength of patience and love." An interesting discussion followed.

Good schools and good Heads have succession plans in place. This ensures that when a visionary leader leaves for any reason, there is someone ready to take over and ensure continuity and fidelity to the long-term ethos and vision of the school. Too often, great institutions wither away when those who founded them or those who most successfully led them move on to something else. It does not have to be that way at all! "What and who comes after me?" is not a taboo question! On the contrary, it is one of the most important questions one can ask and having the fortitude and wisdom to plan for the day after you move on is sometimes just as great a service to the school as the time you spent actively leading it.

In summary, a good school has all the features discussed above. It is a place where everyone is learning and where relationships are nurtured and valued. A good school, much like a flowing river, goes forward on its journey — in pursuit of excellence. We need to understand how to nurture, promote and preserve a space that is happy and enables a journey of discovery, caring and sharing for all. That is a good school!

|CHAPTER 17|

Reflections of a Traveller!

My years in education and teaching have been a voyage of discovery and learning right from my early teaching days as a wide-eyed Krishnamurti follower all the way to receiving the "Bhishma Pitamah" (named after the grand and wise patriarch in the Mahabharata) award from the IPSC after my retirement! I had, of course, chosen to be a teacher in preference to other openings I might have pursued. These decades have given me a lot of pride and joy. I wish to share with my co-voyagers my experiences in Rishi Valley School, Bhavan's Public School, Baroda and The Daly College, Indore.

As a teacher, I invariably made it a point to enter my class with a fresh outlook and not with a mindset that telegraphed a sense of jadedness or a "know-it-all" attitude, which is off-putting. I always felt I was learning while teaching, and I was not afraid to tell students that I did not know something. In any case, children are able to cut through the clutter and see you for what you are very quickly! I learned early in my career that teaching and learning are two sides of the same coin, and they go together. I endeavoured to create an atmosphere where the students felt like they could question me at any time, and I then tried to incorporate relevant and good questions in my book to become part of what I taught and discussed with my students. While equipping the students with the knowledge they need is a primary consideration, making the same lesson all-inclusive and relatable to our own lives enables teaching and learning with a wider perspective.

Then there were the "problem students" who I tried to understand and spend time with one-on-one. I found that in most cases, the so-called "problem students" were crying out for attention and help, and in many cases, teachers or parents at home walled them away and did not truly listen to them or what they were trying to convey. The so-called "problem students" were those whose parents were very busy and could not spend quality time with their children, or those who processed the world a little differently from others, or those who were extremely intelligent but were not able to express themselves, or those who were ignored at home due to other siblings demanding and getting more attention and so on. Often, all that the "problem children" craved was patient hearing and some guidance from someone they trusted. When this happened, the problem vanished, but if they were not listened to and if things festered without outlet and release, they tended to lash out more with time and become hardened. I found that in most cases, with empathy, patience and compassion, we could help them. In some rare cases, we had to have a meeting with the parents and tackle the issue together. We never resorted to so-called "punishment" as it went against everything we stood for, and this was drilled deep into me thanks to my years with Krishnamurti. "Being happy is the beginning of education" as he famously said.

From "problem students", we turn our attention to those dubbed "weak students". My colleagues and I, over the years, developed a framework to grapple with this. We need to start this discussion from a place of understanding. We need to acknowledge that every human being is different. We are not all endowed with the same receptivity, and there are bound to be individual differences that we need to embrace and respect, not single out or pick on! We evolved remedial programmes to help every student to come up to the required level of achievement. This was a point I learned with great benefit to my role as a teacher or principal. I learned that we should never give up on a student, and we are called upon and counted on to ensure that no child is left behind! As time passed, I discovered that every single child has infinite value and limitless potential – the call to action for us is to find every child's inherent strengths and areas that need work. This has to be harnessed with patience and deep warmth. I believed in a simple motto – 'know your student" (KYS), and that was a valuable guiding light for me throughout my years as a teacher and administrator.

Similarly, getting to personally know my students and their stories has been an honour and joy. Once you know someone, where they come from, and what they have gone through thus far, it is far easier to help them realise their true potential and provide some course corrections now and then. We are privileged as teachers to inherently receive the level of trust and confidence from every child, more or less, as well as their parents. How we nurture and grow that bond is in our hands and a responsibility we must not take lightly. Indeed, it is one of the most important things we do! Teaching is a vocation where learning possibilities are limitless! I have shared stories, perspectives, and experiences here in the spirit of humility and love, not with a view to sounding preachy!

As I have learnt over and over, the soul of teaching is a genuine love of children. Each child is unique with their own set of sensibilities, potential and set of strengths. Each student has a distinct flavour about them, and just like we cannot compare a rose and a lily, we should never compare two children, regardless of the temptation or intention. A teacher should always look at children with hope and a positive outlook. Negativity has no place in a school. There are bound to be some "slow learners" just as not everyone walks or runs at the same pace. The teacher has to work with students one-on-one and chart a plan that considers where a child is today, how he/she got there, where he/she needs to get to and thus, what extra or special care he/she needs. Trust in children begets trust and becomes the basis of the relationship. A happy school is one which vibrates with positivity and a sense of possibility and optimism for each new day that dawns.

If I had to summarise what I learned about teaching with a view to passing on these insights to the next generation, I would say the following:

- Love
- Trust
- Together
- Values

The basis of the entire endeavour of the school is LOVE of children and the teachers' passion to teach. The values of the school must be clearly understood by every teacher who makes it his/her life's mission. Sharing and caring are vital in the process. I learned that when I love children, I will learn the other things necessary.

The atmosphere of the school must be filled with TRUST—trust between the children and the teachers, between the teachers and the Head, between the school and the parents and with the community in general. There must be an open relationship for each other to talk about it or any other issue.

There is no place for individualism and "prima donnas" in school education! We are called upon to work TOGETHER in all that we do! Together with children, other staff members, parents and the community we are based in. It takes a proverbial village to raise a child they say. Well, creating and sustaining that village for every child is our job!

And finally, we come to VALUES. There is little point in turning out just academically brilliant students. We have to impart an educational experience that awakens a lifelong hunger for learning, a spirit of consistent pursuit of excellence, a desire to help others (especially those less fortunate) and a healthy ego that is open to receiving feedback. Those leaving the school after a decade or slightly more, even at the high end, will carry with them for the rest of their lives the stamp of what the school stands for! Thus, I have always believed that our children must be strong in academics, play at least one sport, have a taste for music and dance, be voracious readers and participate in all literary and co-curricular activities offered by the school. In today's age of "cut-throat" competition, our school leavers must learn how to win with humility, lose gracefully and leave with grace.

I cannot refrain from sharing a story. In a class full of children from the professional and upper middle classes of society, there was a boy who was there thanks to a scholarship. As it happened, he received admission into the prestigious Indian Institute of Technology (IIT). He came to me and said that he was thinking of declining the offer as his parents could not just afford to send their son to IIT. I asked him to give me a little time before giving him advice. Just then, a Non-Resident Indian (NRI) parent of a child had come to see me, too, and her son had secured admission to the same IIT! I decided to take a chance and asked her if she would be willing to meet the expenses of the other student as a loan! Much to my amazement, she readily agreed and said that she would think that she had one more child of hers at IIT! She said that she was not interested in getting back the money and that I could use it to help another needy student. The "scholarship boy" completed his IIT programme without any worries about finance and landed a good job thereafter. He wrote to us immediately upon graduation, eager to repay in instalments the money spent by his friend's mother. I advised him to keep every instalment with him and use it to help another deserving, needy student and form a chain in which that student would do likewise. Forming a chain of giving brought home all the ingredients we talked about – LOVE, TRUST, TOGETHER and VALUES!

It has been a ride of a lifetime, and I pass the torch on to the next generation of teachers, leaders, and principals! May many of you "write your own book", develop your own toolkit, share often and widely, learn through teaching, love our children and grow with them!

|CHAPTER 18|

My Advice to Students, Parents and Teachers!

I have often been asked what my advice would be! I tend to be a little wary of dispensing broad advice, especially when not everyone is made the same or in the same context. So, rather than advice, I would treat the following more as perspectives or reflections from someone who has travelled on similar roads before as opposed to a roadmap or list of recipes to guarantee success.

To Young Students:

- **Be patient with yourself and those around you** – You might have heard that "hard work always pays off", but nothing worthwhile ever comes without struggle. Also, there are times when hard work does not result in success. However, we define it. That could be a sign that we might be pursuing the wrong goal or, that we are trying too hard to change something when the time is not yet right, or it might simply mean we are approaching the problem wrongly! Set your goals "smartly", as they say – smart goals are specific, measurable, achievable, relevant and time-bound. Then, make a plan that is realistic to achieve those goals, set milestones along the way, and don't be afraid to change course or adjust your plan if you find you are not on the right track.

- **Success also does not always come in a straight line** – The journey is often more complex and nuanced than we imagine it to be. So, embrace the struggle, don't be carried away by your successes and don't take the failures too hard. Both go hand in hand. Learn from your failures and take what you can do better with you! As many who have come before us have said, it is often the failures and struggles that teach us more about the world and ourselves. Also, if one hasn't failed, it just means one hasn't really tried enough!
- **Be authentic!** – Every child is unique and brings a different perspective, voice and colour to this world. Play to your strengths, don't try to be someone you are not and live up to your own promises, not those that others have set for you! We spend far too much time trying to be what others want us to be. You are precious, and so are your unique ways of looking at the world and processing its beauty, complexity and nuance! So, don't let others define being different, being odd or being worthy of exclusion or marginalization. Indeed, our world is so much more beautiful when there is a diversity of thought, expression, art forms, ideas and voices – a rich and beautiful tapestry!
- **Never go to sleep angry with anyone!** – Always be magnanimous and ask for forgiveness if you feel like you wronged someone, however small or large the offence! We are not perfect, but we can control our reactions to the imperfections of others and ourselves! Admitting your mistakes is a sign of strength, not weakness! By the same token, forgive others, especially if they are contrite and

own up to their faults. Begin each day with a note of optimism, hope and a belief that good things will happen ultimately, even if one cannot really shape the final outcome. Most importantly, do your bit by accomplishing what you control!

- **Get enough sleep and maintain a routine** – This might seem obvious or trivial to some, but the importance of sleep and a predictable schedule that your body can count on is increasingly becoming a topic of research and renewed focus. One's energy levels, patience with family, friends and colleagues, focus, clarity and emotional responses can all be affected by how well one slept the night before. It is the magic drug that we can all take and reap the benefits of!
- **Find your unique gift!** – Each of us has something unique and special to offer to those around us and to this world. We need to allow ourselves the time and space to find ourselves and our gifts! Once we do, we tend to be wholesome and fuller human beings, and we also tend to be more comfortable acknowledging our challenges and blind spots. We cannot all be geniuses in mathematics, gifted in sports, or born leaders in business. Why should we try to be someone else's idea of who we are? Each of us deserves to have a nurturing community around us that gives us the time, space and patience to find our special calling!
- **"Play tennis with people better than you!"** – This was advice I received a long time ago, and it stuck with me! In other words, don't be afraid to be surrounded by people

better or smarter than you! In fact, that is how we get better and become the best we are capable of, as opposed to feeling like we know it all. Being around accomplished people has a motivating and galvanizing effect if we take it in the right spirit.

- **"Have the mindset of a marathon runner"** – Sports and running have, in them, many life lessons that one can take away. Foremost among them is cultivating the mindset of a long-distance runner! Compete against your own time and better it, believe in your routines/processes, do all you can in your control and let the results take care of themselves, cultivate perseverance and embrace being with your own thoughts without worrying about the outcome every second!
- **Remember that all bad times and all good times shall pass!** – Nothing lasts forever! So, if you're going through a difficult path in life – on a personal front or in a work or academic context, remind yourself that things will get better if you keep doing what is in your control. And by the same token, if you're experiencing great success, that, too, unfortunately, is not a permanent state! So, enjoy the highs, but don't take them for granted and don't get too down when you hit the lows, for they shall pass!
- **"Walk softly"!** – Always remember we are temporary residents no matter where we live, work, or study! So, always leave a place slightly better than the state you found it in – both physically and in a qualitative sense! Don't leave a dirty room, dormitory, school campus, city, country or world for the next set of people who will

occupy the spaces we sit in today! Be kind, courteous and empathetic to your fellow travellers and also to those who will come after you.

- **The journey matters, often even more than the goal!** – In our results-oriented society, it is easy to forget this essential truth of life, but as I look back and reflect, what I remember vividly is the journey and the co-travellers I shared the path with much more than the peaks I scaled or the destinations I reached! Life is fleeting and goes by much more quickly than we realize, so it is so important to live every moment, be alive to the world around us, fully attend to the people in our lives and cherish the path we are on! Titles, awards, degrees, accolades and other markers of success, such as the size of bank accounts or stock portfolios, fade away in time, and all that remains are memories of the people we associated with and the journeys we undertook! So, make the most of them and have no regrets later in life!
- **Make choices that you can stand behind in time!** – Life will often test you and ask questions of you. You might not get every decision right, but make every effort to think through your choices and why you are making them! Sometimes, taking a shortcut might seem attractive, but often, those decisions will haunt you, and you will wish you could undo them. Try and always do the right thing, even if it means taking the less travelled path, and you will sleep better at night and be comfortable in your skin!

To Parents:

- **Take your role seriously, but not too seriously! –** As parents, we naturally like to think we can shape, influence, inspire, admonish and cajole our children into making choices we approve of and know to be good for them – in small and big matters. While there is a natural need as well as immense value for parental guidance, oversight and involvement in the life of a child, what is also true is that our role has to change over the years as our children are growing up, finding their own voice and place in the sun! We have to learn to suspend judgment, allow our children to exercise free will and learn the lessons of life and the world. We go from being central characters in their life to being supporters in the background – cheering them on, wishing them well and jumping in when called upon or when we see a real need! It is a balance we must strike and one that is critical.
- **"Don't wait for quality time, just spend the time" –** Quality time generally implies time that we set aside in the hope and often wishful anticipation that we can live through a "highlights" reel with our children! We want our children to turn over for the first time or start crawling or walking or say something for the first time in that slot! When they are a little older, we want them to have their first experience or best version of activity with us, confide in us, share something beautiful or unexpected, and so on! Rather than attributing an aspirational or occasionally real grade to the time we are able to spend with our child, what if we simply discard the prefix "quality" and just

give more or all of ourselves more of the time? So much of parenting is about "being there" – being there for our children, being there as fully as we can or at least as much as life allows! The most precious gift we have is the time we get with our children and loved ones! Often, what we most long for when we look back is if it could have lasted longer! So, slow down time, enjoy the most uneventful days, the little routines and rhythms of life with children, for it too shall pass and will leave us with longing and regret when it does!

- **Don't try to teach every lesson of life in real time!** —We often want to relay every life lesson, every nugget of wisdom and every perspective of life in real time to our children. And we are surprised when our children are not receptive to these heartfelt and sincere intentions. We would, however, do well to have a little patience and a healthy dose of humility as we go about our parenting duties! The most powerful lessons are often passed on to our children without actually verbalizing anything. Children observe how we respond to the events of life, the mundane and the dramatic, how we react to people and situations, and the values by which they see us live. Other lessons are internalized by our children at times we least expect them to! So, be patient, don't feel the need to always verbalize and pass commentary, find the right time to have discussions that need to be had and enjoy the travels together!
- **Don't compare children** – Resist the desire to compare your children even if you think you are doing so with

good intent! Also, resist the temptation of comparing your children to those of your friend, co-worker or relative. Every child is different, and we need to be mindful of allowing them the time, space and environment to "find themselves" and be the best versions of themselves they can be.

- **Our children are not vehicles of our unfulfilled ambitions** – As parents, we are protective of our children; we always want the best for our kids and want them to have all the things that we might not have had as children. That is, after all, human nature! What we must try and avoid, though, is putting undue pressure on our children or projecting our own unfulfilled goals and dreams onto them, for they may or may not share those aspirations and ideas of what success looks like! This includes pushing them too hard on career choices, which university they should go to, which subjects are important and so on! We have to learn to detach ourselves from outcomes and be there for them when they need us – serving as sounding board, adviser, coach, motivator, philosopher and most of all, friend!
- **Verbalize and articulate your value system** – While our actions over time play a big role in setting an example for our children, we also need to take the time and verbalize and articulate our value systems from time to time. Whether it is treating people with kindness and empathy, being honest in everything we do, caring for the poor and the homeless, standing up for what is right or being accountable and responsible in what we do and doing

everything with sincerity and hard work – it is important for our children to hear these values articulated. At times, we will fall short as parents, and when we do, it is also important for our kids to hear from us that while we are imperfect at times, our values stay the same, and we continue to strive to be the best versions of ourselves!

- **Guard against passing on a sense of entitlement** – We all find our kids to be adorable, cute, smart, gifted and special! This is an essential part of the journey of each family as our children find their voices and their feet in this world, reassured by the unconditional love and belief we show them. This has value, utility and beauty! What must go hand in hand, though, is keeping ourselves and our children accountable as they grow up! Our children are no less or no more special than other people's children. We must avoid fostering a sense of entitlement in our children, and we have to navigate that balance between unconditional love and being honest with ourselves and our children when they overstep or go too far.
- **"Where all the women are strong, all the men are good-looking, and all the children are above average"** – A well-known radio show would open and close with this line! Over the decades, gender roles, male privilege and what women should and can aspire for have dramatically shifted. As parents, we must be open to new ideas that challenge our long-held ideas and engage in an open and transparent introspection around these sometimes complex issues. We must navigate topics about adolescence and coming of age with maturity, sensitivity

and warmth – particularly guarding against fostering or furthering patriarchy or misplaced sense of masculinity in our boys and resist even the slightest inclination to stereotype or limit the possibilities for our girls while being open to difficult or even awkward conversations about these topics as and when they come up! Girls can be and often are more successful and earn more than boys in today's world and we as parents can help our children be comfortable and secure stakeholders in the more just, equal and open world we envision for them to inhabit!

- **Learn to let go!** – As hard as it is for us as parents, our children have to, sooner or later, learn to live their own lives, make their own decisions about jobs and life partners, live with the consequences of their choices, deal with unkind or mean people, resolve conflicts and learn to recover from heartbreak or loss! It is the way of life, and so we have to learn to set them free once we have given them a firm grounding, a strong sense of values and confidence that they are loved and cherished unconditionally. Every generation deserves their chance to fly, travel to new places and find solutions to the unique challenges of their time!
- **Know when to exit the stage!** – As our kids grow up, we as parents must learn the art of gradually fading from the limelight and yielding to the stage even as we assume the role of enablers, cheerleaders and background support! This is hard for us to do as we are used to being the ones controlling things, making decisions, and looking after those for whom we are responsible. This is a change each

of us has to be comfortable with and one that we should make with ease and grace!

- **It takes a village to raise a child!** — We must remember that the nuclear family structure we find ourselves in has not been the way forever and is a relatively new concept! Living in a fragmented setup where each set of parents takes care of their children leads to challenges of various kinds for both parents and the children! Being part of a larger community, be it extended family or a setup involving other friends, like-minded parents, and children, is not only easier for everyone concerned, but it also leads to better outcomes for the child in the long run. Learning how to share, spending time with others, watching grandparents as they navigate their mortality and ageing process, making compromises, dealing with personalities of all types and appreciating that we are part of a larger society are all valuable life lessons best inculcated in children early on!

To Teachers:

- **Don't be envious of children more gifted than you!** — As teachers, we come across children with a wide range of abilities and talents. And often, we will find ourselves in the company of students whose intellect and ability to reason and think surpasses ours. They might have read more widely than us, have an inherent ability to solve complex problems faster than us or might see shortcomings in the claims we make while we are teaching their class. When we come across such children, we should cherish them, find ways to challenge them positively and provide them with resources that enable them to grow even more! We should guard against stifling their creativity or lashing out when we are challenged. We should feel blessed to have students of all capabilities, backgrounds and personalities, for this is what makes for a lively and colourful classroom!

- **What you say matters, but how you say it does even more!** – Providing honest and thoughtful feedback is an essential part of the process and one that we must take seriously. Whether it is a pat on the back, a pep talk or a longer conversation on ways to do better, we owe it to our students to be forthcoming and transparent, for that is how growth and learning happen! What is equally critical, though, is how we provide this feedback. Yelling at them in the presence of others, or harshly criticising them, or comparing them unfavourably to their classmates can cause a child to be affected in ways much more profound and lost lasting than one can guess. Public appreciation (but at the expense of nobody else!) and critical/tougher conversations in private work well, in my view, but each teacher must come up with their own approach to these situations, keeping in mind at all times that it is young and impressionable minds we are dealing with!
- **Never give up on any child** – Every child deserves a second chance, especially if offering one is within our control! We have all been the beneficiaries of people in our lives who bet on us when we were down, lent a helping hand when we were at our weakest or encouraged us when our self-confidence was low. As teachers, we must

always believe that every student of ours will go on to write their own unique life story and deserve a second chance when they stumble or fall short, not our scorn or harsh finality of judgment! Not giving up on our children does not mean we don't hold them accountable for striving for excellence or living up to our values. What it simply means is to be aware that they are not perfect, just as we are not! And that awareness will allow us to offer them empathetic support when they need it, and often, it is those second chances we enable that go on to produce the brightest minds and best leaders of the future!

- **Apply rules consistently but compassionately** – This was something my father taught me when I was a young boy. Rules are important, and we must respect them. As teachers, we must also be compassionate when we are enforcing them. We must listen to their side of events, take into consideration any context or accentuating circumstances, remind them about why the rules exist the way they do and arrive at a fair and thoughtful decision. We must also strive to find creative ways to allow children to learn from their mistakes and grow from the experience. Children are not bad, but they might make bad decisions or show poor judgment occasionally!
- **Be open to feedback and own your mistakes!** – As teachers, we must constantly get better at how and what we teach. And for that, we need to get feedback from our students. The format of how we seek and get feedback can vary. It can be anonymous, written, informal, verbal, or somewhere in between. When we do receive feedback, we

must treat it with respect and make tangible changes if needed. We must also be open to admitting our mistakes, learning from them and putting in the work to improve. This is how we set the tone for our students and show them that their opinions carry weight. Just as our feedback makes our children better, we, too, must be secure enough to seek input from our students and be open to doing things differently when it is warranted.

- **Keep yourself updated and abreast of the latest in your field** – The world around us is changing, and so is our collective understanding of it today and, in some cases, going back in time. This is also true of subjects that we teach in the classroom. There are better and newer ways of teaching concepts, state-of-the-art research on the art and science of teaching, as well as, in some cases, an updated understanding of topics that we might have taught for decades in some cases! It is imperative that we keep ourselves abreast of what is transpiring in our respective fields and in the field of education in general. This can take various forms – from "INSET" (in Service Training) to taking a class online to attending a conference to reading the latest publications. We would be doing our students a disservice if we treat the syllabus and how we teach it as if they are beyond change.
- **Remember that teaching and learning go together!** – We must never forget that in this journey of school education that we chose to pursue, we, too, are lifelong learners! As we teach a new topic in class, let us approach it with the freshness of someone doing so for the very first time!

Allow yourself to be excited if your students grasp what you are trying to convey, genuinely happy if they engage deeper in the subject and want more discussion and step back and appreciate if a student points out something or brings out a perspective you did not hear before! Good teachers keep discovering more depth, new nuances and better ways to see a problem in the subjects they teach! And it is this constant symphony between learning and teaching that keeps education fresh, interesting and lively!

- **Earn the respect of your children** – There is a belief in some circles that, as teachers, we must demand that our classrooms observe "pin-drop silence" and that we receive "100% attention" (as we define it). Often, this is referred to as "discipline". Instead, we must aim to create a happy, vibrant, diverse, and spirited space where respect is earned and mutual – both between the teacher and the student and between fellow students. Fear of teachers or consequences does not inspire and will not produce leaders of the future! On the contrary, it allows a culture where compliance and approval-seeking get the better of true learning or growth! We must create an environment where each student is comfortable speaking up, asking questions, contributing to discussions, requesting that a topic be revisited, and respecting each other's opinions, even if we disagree. At the same time, we must be mindful that rules and a general sense of decorum must apply. That is true respect!
- **Encourage our children to read!** – Just as we teach our children to read, write, perform addition or subtraction or

solve equations, we must also constantly emphasise to them the value of reading wide books of various types. As educationists, we cannot possibly teach our students everything merely during our classroom lectures, lab sessions or as part of homework. We must creatively inculcate a love for books in our children, for this will serve them well for decades to come. Be it classic or modern/contemporary literature, fiction or non-fiction, autobiographies or adventure thrillers – let them lap it all up! We can set up a book club, reward the child who reads the most books over a summer or devote the last 15 minutes of the Friday afternoon class we teach to have children summarise their latest read and what they took away from it. This may or may not have anything to do with our direct subject at hand, but it will go a long way in preparing students for a lifetime of experiences ahead.

- **Tomorrow is full of possibilities!** – We must be steadfastly and unconditionally optimistic about the future of every child that crosses our path as teachers! Every child is born with inherent value and has their own unique strengths to enrich this world, and we must be empathetic guides in the part of their life journey that they have entrusted to us. We must elevate the discourse and inspire our children to be the best versions of themselves! We must teach them to take disappointments in their stride and not get carried away by success either. A relentless pursuit of excellence and a belief in a better tomorrow must be at the core of all we do as teachers!

AFTERWORDS

VETERAN'S NOTE

Acceptance speech by Dr. M.V. Prasad on being conferred "Bhishma Pitamaha Award" by IPSC on 10th January 2022

I would like to thank Honourable Union Minister for Education, Shri Dharmendra Pradhanji, Mrs. Nishi Misra, Chairperson, Dr. Jagpreet Singh, Honorary Secretary, Mr. Anil Shanna, Joint Secretary, and dear colleagues. I feel humbled and honoured to have been conferred the "Bhishma Pitamaha Award." I thank Mr. B.K. Sood, for proposing my name and all office bearers and colleagues for unanimously supporting the proposition. My deep gratitude goes to you all. I accept the honour in all humility. I feel we are at a crossroads, having to pass through one phase after the other of COVID with various strains. Because of this hydra-headed conundrum, as it were, schools are asked to open and shut. Everyone talks of the damage caused to the economy, which is indeed true, but very few talk of the academic damage caused to the students, which can have far-reaching consequences for the future. But, as teachers, let's not bemoan the suffering thrust on us but take it as a challenge to usher in a new order. Let's build new bridges to the future for moving from post-industrial to post-COVID education by investing in human potential. Education is honouring the innate intelligence of every pupil and bringing the best out of every child. In this endeavour, a crucial factor is the right relationships. Our relationship with students should be based on compassion; it should be friendly, not familiar, approachable, not cheap, and always dignified, and there should be freedom not to do what one wants to do but to do the right thing always. Let's help each child of today grow into a responsible citizen of the world.

I think digital schools have come to stay, where technology is widely used. I suggest we offer blended learning, that is, use technology to the extent needed instead of getting drowned in technology. Virtual schools have come into existence, though there is an element of unreality in them. Let's remember, friends, technology is a useful tool, but let it not become the master. We are the masters, and technology is only a tool for us to use intelligently. We must make constant efforts for teachers and heads to continue to learn and polish our skills. As Dr. Jagpreet Singh and Satya Nadella said, in some other context, what we need is "skilling, re-skilling, up-skilling." In the UK, they place great emphasis on this, and they call it "INSET (In-Service Training of Teachers)." This is vital in the field of education, though sadly, we do not give enough emphasis to this in our schools. In fact, in the UK, they have gone a step further and have started a National Institute of Educational Leadership at Nottingham.

Our guiding principle in all our endeavours should be, I feel, DHARMA, which is a loaded word. Let's go into it for a couple of minutes. The first word of the first shloka in the Bhagwad Gita is DHARMA. The last word of the last shloka is MAMA – 'MAMA DHARMA, which means everyone must perform his or her DHARMA, and then the world will be all right. DHARMA is an all-inclusive word which could mean duty, right action, humility, compassion, straight path. The DHARMA of the teacher, the student and the school should always be remembered. When we go to one of our member schools, I hear the teachers and the students say, "Sir, this is done in our school, or this is not done in our school". That is the DHARMA of the school, which is its ethos. In the Marwari language, if I can quote one line, there is a beautiful saying, which is "Dharam rehasi, rehasi dhara", which means, "Where DHARMA is preserved, the Earth (Dhara) is preserved."

In the Merchant of Venice, Portia pleads with Shylock in the court to show mercy to Antonio and while delivering the beautiful speech, "the quality of mercy is not strained", she says, "it is an attribute to God himself." But Shylock refuses to do it, for which he suffers the consequences later. In a different way, this idea is encapsulated in a very simple poem, which we all would have studied as junior school students, "The Village Blacksmith." I quote a few lines from that:

"Toiling, rejoicing, sorrowing,
Onward through life, he goes;
Each morning sees some task begun,
Each evening sees it close;
Something attempted, something done,
He earned a night's repose."

You earn a night's repose; we can't take it for granted. That is the DHARMA of the so-called illiterate village blacksmith, but his skills go with this DHARMA. The foundation of a school should thus be based on DHARMA. Now, I come to thank my friends and my seniors. I respectfully dedicate this award to the world teacher and great philosopher, J. Krishnamurti, with whom I had the opportunity to work for 19 years at Rishi Valley, and to my late father, an educationist himself, for inspiring me to go to Rishi Valley and become a teacher, which paved a way of life for me, which I am very very happy about. In the IPSC, I acknowledge the guidance received from seniors like Mr. Shomie Das and Dr. S.D. Singh. Mr. B.K. Sood has been my mentor and has supported and guided me at every stage of my growth. When he became the Chairman of the IPSC, he unhesitatingly appointed me as the Secretary of IPSC during the Golden Jubilee celebrations. Working with him has been a valuable learning experience for me. I acknowledge Dr. M.P. Chhaya, who gave me an opportunity to come up, by involving me in a number of committees and commissions, and most importantly, in founding the Navodaya Vidyalayas, to which he gave the academic framework and that was a great learning experience for me. As you are aware, my friends, the Navodaya Vidyalayas are some of the very best schools in the country today.

My deep gratitude goes to all members of the IPSC for the honour they have given me. When Mr. B.K. Sood suggested my name, Mrs. Nishi Misra, Dr. Jagpreet Singh and Mr. Anil Sharma responded with alacrity and followed it up with the staunch support of all the colleagues. I am indeed deeply indebted to all of you.

I wish to end by quoting a short prayer in Sanskrit, which I am very fond of:

"Sarve bhavantu sukhinah,
Sarve santu niramayah,
Sarve bhadrani pasyantu,
Ma kascit dhukhabhag bhavet.
Santih! Santih! Santih!"

In English, it means — "Let all here be happy. Let's all see the face of happiness. Let no one be unhappy. Peace! Peace! Peace!"

Thank you.

Dr. M. V. Prasad

IPSC Honorary Member & IPSC Trust Member

Biography of Dr. M.V. Prasad

M.V. Prasad has a Master's Degree in English and a Bachelor of Education degree, both from the University of Mysore. He was awarded a Doctor of Education degree (honoris causa) by the De Montfort University, Leicester, England. He worked at Rishi Valley School for nineteen years as English teacher, house master, senior master and later as Head master. He attended J. Krishnamurti's talks and discussion meetings in India and England and had the benefit of having in formal interactions with him on many occasions. He was also a member of the Krishnamurti Foundation of India for a term (1978-80). Dr. Prasad, Retired as Principal of The Daly College, Indore, and before that he was Principal of Bhavan's V.M. Public School, Baroda as well as Principal of The Indian School, Bahrain (A.G). He was the Chairman of the Indian Public Schools Conference. Widely travelled, Dr. Prasad has been a speaker at a number of international conferences of Principals held in Geneva, Sydney, Boston, Helsinki, Birmingham etc. He was a member of the Governing body of the CBSE. He is an International Member of the National Association of Secondary School Principals, USA, a Fellow of the Secondary Heads Association, UK and a Fellow of the Royal Society of Arts, London. Dr. Prasad and his wife Sheela now live in Mumbai